THE SEVEN-BRANCHED LIGHT

A Reading Guide and Index to

The Universal Jewish Encyclopedia

An Authoritative and Popular Presentation of
Jews and Judaism Since the Earliest Times

ISAAC LANDMAN, D.D., *Editor*

Arranged
for
convenient
research
and
reference
by readers,
students,
teachers

Especially
designed
to
stimulate
and
facilitate
adult
Jewish
education

Compiled by
SIMON COHEN, D.D.
Director of Research

UNIVERSAL JEWISH ENCYCLOPEDIA CO., INC., NEW YORK

TABLE OF CONTENTS

INTRODUCTION

FOR THE PAST decade the Jewish people has been tragically thrust into the very foreground of world history and it will continue to remain there during the coming post-war reconstruction. Authoritative information about Jews and Judaism, therefore, is of vital concern to Christian and Jew alike. To remedy the destruction wrought by hate and falsehood, to break down the barriers created by malice and ignorance, accurate and authentic information is the indispensable instrument. Jews particularly ought to be thoroughly acquainted with their own history, religion, lore and culture, not only for their own spiritual development and understanding, but also to meet with intelligence and vigor the problems that face the Jewish people as a whole.

It was for these purposes that the editors of this encyclopedia have made it their goal to produce a Jewish encyclopedia which is truly *universal*—in the sense that it is thoroughly comprehensive and able to instruct not merely the learned but also the average individual who seeks information. For this reason it has been written in clear and easily flowing style, yet sacrificing nothing of accuracy or authority in the process, maintaining a scholarly level, yet possessing a wide popular appeal. Thousands of new facts have been sought out and assembled in order to meet the questions that are being asked every day, and copious illustrations are furnished to give knowledge by visual instruction.

However, the editors feel that a further step is necessary before the student can make full use of the accumulated information crammed within the ten volumes of the encyclopedia. Individual topics are easy to find; but for a thorough knowledge on many fields of interest about Jews and Judaism some guide is necessary and some reading plan is imperative. Accordingly, this study book and guide has been compiled as an index to the most important articles in a number of fields where information has been and is constantly being sought by Jew and non-Jew alike. It is aimed to help the child to do his own reading and study, to assist the teacher in presenting subjects, to encourage pupils to do their own research, and, on a still higher level, to provide a series of syllabi for adult classes and readers.

The 100 outlines contained within this book are grouped under seven heads into which the accumulated information about the Jews naturally falls: history, literature, religion, Jewish life, Jews and non-Jews, general subjects, and Jewish contributions to civilization. The outlines contain more than 5,000 articles—about half of those in the encyclopedia, with more than two-thirds of its entire text. These articles are arranged in a suitable order for reading, with introductions and explanatory notes. Volume and page numbers of every article listed are added for the convenience of the reader, and illustrations elsewhere in the encyclopedia are duly indicated.

To save space, the titles of articles are occasionally abbreviated, but in such a way that the reader will have no difficulty in finding them.

Some outlines (such as those on JEWISH LITERATURE) are general surveys of a subject, subordinate topics of which (such as HEBREW and JEWISH LITERATURE) are treated in subsequent outlines. Each outline is constructed to be a complete reading course in itself; and since the teachings and practices of Judaism are closely united, in many cases the same article will be listed under more than one outline.

The student will occasionally find differing and even contradictory points of view expressed by the writers of various articles; he must bear in mind that each age of Jewish life has reinterpreted Judaism in the light of its own need and in terms of its own environment, and that in so vast a field as that of Jewish history and religion there are bound to be different interpretations of the same facts.

A number of outlines give lists of individuals of note in various fields. Limitations of space prevent the citing of every name mentioned in the encyclopedia, save in a few instances. In some spheres of endeavor, such as medicine, music, public office and art, there are hundreds of individuals whose biographies appear in the encyclopedia. In all these lists, therefore, selections from the larger group have been made on the basis of the combined judgments of experts in the various fields.

Each outline has been drawn up as a complete unit in itself, and no attempt has been made to give them a uniform length. However, the longer outlines, for example those on Jewish History, the United States, Bible, or Jews in Literature, are so demarcated that they can easily be divided into convenient sections for reading or study. The student who desires to delve more deeply into subjects of his choice will find suggestions for further study in the course of reading the major articles listed in the outlines; he is also referred to the numerous suggestions for further reading and the abundant literature appended to these articles.

Dr. Simon Cohen, the Director of Research, who has contributed much to the planning and development of the encyclopedia, as well as undertaking the major work in preparing its text, has prepared the 100 outlines which constitute this book. His comprehensive knowledge, his careful analysis and arrangement of each topic, and his illuminating notations make this "Seven Branched Light" a constructive contribution to Jewish education and to the promotion of Jewish knowledge, for which numerous readers, students and teachers will be most grateful to him. We are confident that this study book will serve as a key to unlock the treasures of the encyclopedia so that whoever seeks may find within its pages whatever he desires of information, illumination and inspiration.

ISAAC LANDMAN
Editor in Chief

Brooklyn, N. Y.
Eve of Rosh Hashanah, 1943.

I desire to take this occasion to return thanks to those who have contributed to the making of this book: to Isaac Landman, to whom the original idea of the work is due; to Louis Rittenberg and other of the editors, who have made valuable suggestions; to Abraham I. Shinedling, for assistance in the preparation of the manuscript; and to the many seekers of information, whose very questions furnished most useful indications of the type of knowledge that was sought and the most suitable paths through which it could be found.

SIMON COHEN

ABBREVIATIONS

The following abbreviations, in parentheses, are used for the names of countries in the outlines that follow:

A	. . . . Austria	Ho	. . . . Holland	Ru	. . . . Russia
Aus	. . . . Australia	Hu	. . . . Hungary	Sc	. . . . Scotland
Be	. . . . Belgium	I	. . . . Italy	S Af	. . . . South Africa
Bu	. . . . Bulgaria	ill	. . . . illustration	S	. . . . Spain
C	. . . . Canada	Ir	. . . . Ireland	Sw	. . . . Sweden
Cz	. . . . Czechoslovakia	M	. . . . Mexico	Swi	. . . . Switzerland
D	. . . . Denmark	N	. . . . Norway	Sy	. . . . Syria
E	. . . . England	P	. . . . Palestine	T	. . . . Turkey
F	. . . . France	Po	. . . . Poland	US	. . . . United States
G	. . . . Germany	Pt	. . . . Portugal		
Gr	. . . . Greece	Ro	. . . . Roumania		

PART I: HISTORY

OUTLINE 1:

JEWISH HISTORY IN GENERAL

The worldwide distribution of the Jewish people and the differences in their status in various countries and at different periods make it impossible to present a uniform and continuous history of the Jews. The subject must be approached from numerous angles. The articles that deal principally with the settlement of the Jews in the several continents are

Asia 1:546-51
Africa §1. 1:107-9

Europe 4:194-95
American Continent 1:225-35

The following articles, which deal with certain aspects and specific features of Jewish history which cannot be delimited by geographic area or period of time, should be studied as background material.

Migrations of the
Jews 7:543-56
State 10:21-23
Self-Government
9:466

Taxation 10:180-82
Tribunals 10:305-6
Assimilation 1:556-61

OUTLINE 2:

JEWISH HISTORY BY PERIODS

The simplest and best way to study Jewish history is to divide it into certain specific periods which are dominated by distinctive Jewish centers or characterized by certain general movements. In the earliest stages of Jewish history such periods follow each other clearly in chronological order. Beginning with the period of the Dispersion, however, when rival Jewish centers arise in different parts of the world and under different political conditions, it becomes necessary to take each center separately, although in many cases the divisions overlap chronologically and geographically. Each of these periods is presented in this outline with its chief political events, its social and religious life and institutions, and through biographies of its great leaders.

A general outline of all the periods is found in **HISTORY** 5: 398-99. *The individual periods can then be taken up as follows:*

1. The Building of the Nation
(about 1500 to 1000 B.C.E.)

a. The Traditional Beginnings

Abraham 1:35-36
Isaac 5:587-88
Jacob 6:5-7
Joseph 6:187-88
Egypt 4:6-10

Moses 8:1-6
Wilderness
10:519-20
Joshua 6:202-4

b. The Land of Canaan

Palestine 8:347-55   Canaan 2:651

Nations Displaced by the Israelites

Amalek, Amalekites
1:218
Amorites 1:279-80
Hittites 5:402-3
Hivites 5:403

Girgashites 4:614
Perizzites 8:458
Anakim 1:293
Rephaim 9:135

A special problem is furnished by references in Egyptian records to a people which settled in the country about 1400 B.C.E. Habiri 5:144-45.

c. Settlement and Early Struggles of the Israelites

Twelve Tribes 10:330 (there are separate articles on each of the tribes)

Ehud 4:21
Deborah 3:504
Gideon 4:606-7

Jephthah 6:58
Samson 9:341-44
Samuel 9:345-47

Nations with Which the Israelites Were at War

Ammon, Ammonites
1:276-77
Ishmaelites 5:609-10
Midian, Midianites
7:537-38

Moab, Moabites
7:602-3
Philistines 8:489-90

d. Cult Objects and Institutions

Tabernacle
10:152 53
Ark of the Covenant
1:478-79
Ephod 4:134
Teraphim 10:199

High Place 5:357-58
Cities of Refuge
3:216
Priests 8:642-44
Elders 4:46

2. The Period of the Kingdom
(1000 to 586 B.C.E.)

a. Political History

Israel 5:613-15   Judah 6:219-22

b. Nations and Rulers with Which the Israelites Came into Contact

Jebus, Jebusites
6:50-51
Phoenicians
8:517-19
Edom, Edomites
3:628
Shishak 9:511
Aram 1:448-50

Ethiopia 4:182
Assyria 1:561-67
Tiglath-pileser 10:250
Scythians 9:449
Chaldeans 3:108-9
Babylonia 2:9-12
Arabs §1. 1:442-43

c. Religious Institutions and Movements

Temple 10:193-97

Prophets and
Prophecy 8:658-64

d. **Important Leaders**

David 3:475-82   Isaiah 5:601-4
Elijah 4:71-74   Jeremiah 6:60-65
Amos 1:280-82

3. The Babylonian Exile
(586 to 539 B.C.E.)

Babylonia 2:12   Evil-merodach 4:200
Exile, Babylonian   Belshazzar 2:154
    4:209-12   Ezekiel 4:219-23
Nebuchadrezzar II   Deutero-Isaiah
    8:139   5:604-5 (in Isaiah)

4. The Persian Period
(539 to 331 B.C.E.)

a. **Foreign Rulers**

Persia 8:460-62   Artaxerxes II 1:500
Cyrus the Great   Bagoas 2:32
    3:438   Artaxerxes III
Darius 3:471   1:500-1
Artaxerxes I 1:500

b. **New Institutions and Movements**

Synagogue 10:119-30
Temple 10:194-95 (The Second Temple)
Samaritans 9:335-36

c. **Other Jewish Settlements**

Babylonia 2:12   Elephantine 4:64-65

d. **Jewish Leaders**

Zerubbabel 10:640-41   Nehemiah 8:146
Ezra 4:226-27   Simon the Just 9:543

5. The Greek Period (331 to 165 B.C.E.)

a. **Foreign Rulers**

Alexander the Great   Seleucidae 9:465
    1:171-72   Antiochus III 1:339
Ptolemies 9:21-22   Antiochus IV 1:339

b. **Other Countries of Jewish Settlement**

Babylonia 2:12-13   Egypt 4:11
Persia 8:462   Ethiopia 4:182-84
Syria 10:135

c. **New Institutions and Movements**

Diaspora 3:560   Hellenism 5:306-7
Sanhedrin 9:361-63   Hasideans 5:237
Onias, Temple of
    8:301

d. **Jewish Leaders**

Jaddua 6:26   Jason 6:42
Tobiads 10:258   Menelaus 7:483-84
Onias 8:300-1

6. The Hasmonean Period
(165 to 37 B.C.E.)

a. **The Struggle for Independence**

Judea 6:251-54   Jonathan Maccabeus
Maccabees 7:260   6:181-82
Judas Maccabeus   Simon Thassi
    6:248-50   9:543-44

b. **The Hasmonean Dynasty**

Hyrcanus I 5:518   Salome Alexandra
Aristobulus I 1:473   9:321
Alexander Jannaeus   Aristobulus II 1:473
    1:173   Hyrcanus II 5:518-19
    Antigonus 1:336

c. **Rulers or Generals of Other Countries**

Antiochus V 1:339   Antiochus VII
Alexander Balas   1:339-40
    1:170   Antiochus IX 1:340
    Pompey 8:585-86

d. **Other Countries near Judea**

Edom, Edomites   Nabateans 8:79
    3:628

e. **New Movements**

Sadducees 9:308-9   Essenes 4:167-68
Pharisees 8:473-76

f. **Other Jewish Settlements**

Babylonia 2:13   Italy 5:625
Greece 5:91

7. Loss of Independence
(37 B.C.E. to 70 C.E.)

a. **Rulers of Palestine**

Judea 6:254   Procurators 8:652-54
Herod 5:325-26   Pontius Pilate 8:586
Herodians 5:327   Agrippa I 1:128
Archelaus 1:466   Agrippa II 1:128
Antipas 1:340   Berenice 2:196
Herodias 5:327

b. **Roman Leaders and Emperors**

Caesar, Caius Julius   Claudius 3:219
    2:622-23   Nero 8:151
Augustus 1:615   Vespasian 10:410
Caligula 2:645   Titus 10:257

c. **Other Countries**

Egypt 4:11   Anilai and Asinai
Persia 8:462   1:319
Parthians 8:404   Adiabene 1:85

d. **New Movements**

Zealots 10:630-31   Christianity
Messianic   3:177-86
    Movements 7:505

e. **Jewish Leaders**

Hillel I 5:362-63   Johanan ben Zakkai
Philo 8:495-96   6:164-66

8. The Mishnaic-Talmudic Period (70 to 500)

a. **Roman Emperors**

Trajan 10:291   Alexander Severus
Hadrian 5:151   1:173
Antoninus Pius   Diocletian 3:568
    1:413   Constantine I 3:338
Marcus Aurelius   Julian 6:265-66
    7:347-48   Arcadius 1:456
Caracalla 3:36-37

The outlines which follow deal with the histories of the individual countries and the communities there. In each outline the order followed is: 1. the history of the country; 2. supplementary articles on rulers, noteworthy characters or institutions; 3. the history of the communities, arranged in geographical order.

OUTLINE 3: UNITED STATES

The history of the Jews in the United States is largely that of individual communities, and presents no integrated picture. This section, accordingly, begins with a number of topics which either record the migrations of the Jews or trace their relations with the Federal Government.

A brief account of the settlement of the Jews in the country is given in

AMERICAN CONTINENT 1:231-34, 234-35

The relationship of Jews and Judaism to American ideals and to American political parties, as well as the intervention of the United States in behalf of Jews abroad, are treated in

UNITED STATES 10:349-51

The following articles deal with the relationships of presidents and important leaders of the United States and the Jews:

Franklin, Benjamin 4:413-14
Washington, George 10:470-71
Adams, John 1:81
Jefferson, Thomas 6:51-52
Madison, James 7:268-69
Van Buren, Martin 10:392
Lincoln, Abraham 7:65-68
Grant, Ulysses Simpson 5:83-84
Harrison, Benjamin 5:222
Roosevelt, Theodore 9:198-99
Hay, John 5:253-54
Taft, William Howard 10:155-56
Wilson, Woodrow 10:526-27
Coolidge, Calvin 3:352
Hoover, Herbert Clark 5:452-53
Roosevelt, Franklin Delano 9:195-98
Willkie, Wendell Lewis 10:523

The following articles deal with states and communities of the United States:

A. New England States

1. **Maine 7:296-97**

Lewiston 7:27-28   Portland 8:604

2. **New Hampshire 8:165-66**

3. **Vermont 10:405-6**

Burlington 2:605

4. **Massachusetts 7:401-6**

Boston 2:481-84   Brockton 2:537
  (illus. 3:85)   Fall River 4:241-42
Revere 9:149   New Bedford 8:163-4
Lynn 7:252-53   Lowell 7:217-18
Salem 9:319   Worcester 10:571-72
Peabody 8:418   Springfield 10:17-18
Quincy 9:46   Pittsfield 8:547

5. **Rhode Island 9:152-53**

Providence 9:10-12
Newport 8:213-15 (illus. 1:232, 234)

A unique institution in the latter town is described in United Company of Spermaceti Candlers 10:347-48

6. **Connecticut 3:332-34**

Stamford 10:19-20   Meriden 7:493
Norwalk 8:241-42   New Britain 8:164-65
Bridgeport 2:528   Hartford 5:230-32
New Haven 8:166-67   New London 8:170
Waterbury 10:475-76   Norwich 8:244-45

B. Middle Atlantic States

1. **New York 8:196-205 (including Long Island 8:200-5)**

(illus. 10:128)
New York City 8:175-96 (illus. 1:112, 220, 234, 252, 274, 475; 2:126; 3:78, 85; 4:265, 427; 5:299, 469; 6:132, 143-45; 9:422; 10: 126, 595)
Brooklyn 2:544-57 (illus. 9:625)
Ellis Island 4:85-86 (illus. 1:237)
Mount Vernon 8:24-25
Yonkers 10:606-7 (illus. 2:426)
Port Chester 8:602   Troy 10:314
New Rochelle 8:173   Schenectady 9:395-96
White Plains 10:510   Utica 10:385-86
Spring Valley 10:16   Binghamton 2:355
Newburgh 8:209-10   Syracuse 10:133-34
Monticello 7:634   Elmira 4:88-89
Poughkeepsie 8:610   Rochester 9:177-78
Kingston 6:395   Buffalo 2:583-84
Albany 1:157-58

2. **New Jersey 8:167-69**

Newark 8:206-9   Elizabeth 4:81-82
Jersey City 6:69-70   Linden 7:69
Bayonne 2:121-22   Plainfield 8:550-51
Orange 8:318   Perth Amboy 8:466-67
South Orange 9:669   New Brunswick 8:165
West Orange 10:507   Trenton 10:300-3
Union City 10:346   Camden 2:649
Passaic 8:407-8   Atlantic City 1:600
Paterson 8:412-13   Woodbine 10:570-71
  (illus. 2:87)

3. **Pennsylvania 8:426-33**

Philadelphia 8:476-84   Reading 9:89
  (illus. 3:601; 4:225) Lancaster 6:520
Easton 3:618-19   Harrisburg 5:220-22
Scranton 9:447-48   Aaronsburg 1:8
Wilkes-Barre   Pittsburgh 8:545-47
  10:521-22   Erie 4:152-53
Allentown 1:188

4. Delaware 3:516-17
    Wilmington 10:525-26

5. Maryland 7:391-93
    Baltimore 2:53-58 (illus. 3:235)

6. Washington, D. C. 10:465-68
    (illus. 7:41)

7. Virginia 10:426-28
    Norfolk 8:236-37   Newport News 8:215
    Portsmouth 8:606   Richmond 9:159-60

8. West Virginia 10:507-9

C. Southeastern States

1. North Carolina 8:237-40

2. South Carolina 9:663-65
    Charleston 3:114-18 (illus. 10:127)
    Sumter 10:102-3

3. Georgia 4:535-39
    Savannah 9:384-85   Atlanta 1:599-600
      (illus. after 10:124)

4. Florida 4:343-44
    Jacksonville 6:4-5   Tampa 10:168-69
    Miami 7:528

5. Tennessee 10:197-98
    Knoxville 6:421-22   Nashville 8:102
    Chattanooga 3:122-23   Memphis 7:462-64

6. Alabama 1:152-54
    Birmingham 2:367-68   Mobile 7:603-4
    Montgomery 7:632-33   (illus. 10:129)

7. Mississippi 7:586-88
    (illus. 10:129)

D. Middle West States

1. Ohio 8:287-91
    Steubenville 10:63   Columbus 3:311-12
    Cleveland 3:220-23   Toledo 10:262-63
      (illus. 2:423;   Dayton 3:493-94
      10:127)   Cincinnati 3:205-11
    Youngstown 10:608   (illus. 5:282-83;
    Akron 1:151-52   7:41; 10:127)
      (illus. 1:647)

2. Kentucky 6:362-63
    (illus. 10:129-30)
    Louisville 7:209-10

3. Michigan 7:534-37
    Detroit 3:545-49   Grand Rapids
    Flint 4:329-30   5:82-83

4. Indiana 5:557-58
    Fort Wayne 4:358-59   Terre Haute
    Indianapolis 5:558-59   10:199-200
    South Bend 9:666-67   Evansville 4:195-96
    Gary 4:514-15

5. Wisconsin 10:532-36
    Milwaukee 7:565-67   Madison 7:268

6. Illinois 5:538-39
    Chicago 3:134-48   Peoria 8:434
      (illus. 1:220; 3:85) Springfield 10:16-17
    Waukegan 10:477-78   Rock Island 9:179

E. Southwestern States

1. Missouri 7:589-91
    Saint Louis 9:312-15
    Kansas City 6:306-8 (illus. 3:87)
    St. Joseph 9:312

2. Arkansas 1:480-81
    (illus. 2:424; 10:129)
    Little Rock 7:139

3. Louisiana 7:206-9
    New Orleans 8:171-73   Shreveport 9:519-20

4. Kansas 6:305-6
    (illus. 2:451)
    Wichita 10:511-13

5. Oklahoma 8:291-92
    Tulsa 10:322   Oklahoma City 8:292

6. Texas 10:203-8
    Galveston 4:502-5   Fort Worth 4:359
    Houston 5:474-77   San Antonio 9:353-54
    Waco 10:437-38   El Paso 4:42-43
    Dallas 3:447-48

F. Western States

1. Minnesota 7:572
    Saint Paul 9:315-16   Duluth 3:608-9
    Minneapolis 7:571-72

2. Iowa 5:582-85
    Des Moines 3:542-43   Sioux City 9:558

3. North Dakota 8:240-41

4. South Dakota 9:669

5. Nebraska 8:137-39
    Omaha 8:297-99   Lincoln 7:64

6. Montana 7:627-28

7. Wyoming 10:581-82

8. Colorado 3:304-5
    Denver 3:538-39

9. New Mexico 8:170-71

G. Far Western States

1. Idaho 5:534

2. Utah 10:385
    Salt Lake City 9:329-30

3. Arizona 1:474-75
    Phoenix 8:519

H. Territories

For other United States territories, see under WEST INDIES, CENTRAL AMERCA and the FAR EAST. The agricultural colonies in the United States are treated under

OUTLINE 4: CANADA

Jews first settled in Canada about the middle of the 18th century. A few of them played important parts in the English conquest in 1759 and in the following years. The numbers of the Jewish settlers were comparatively small until the last decade of the 19th century, and the chief Jewish settlements are in the areas around the Great Lakes and the upper St. Lawrence River. The general article on the subject is

The communities, arranged according to geographical location, are

The agricultural colonies in Canada are treated under

OUTLINE 5: WEST INDIES

The Jewish settlements in the West Indies are of interest because they furnished a springboard for the Jewish settlements in North America.

It was in the West Indies that Jews first set foot on American soil, and through the 18th century the Jewish settlements there were prosperous and influential. Jamaica, in the West Indies, was the first place to emancipate the Jews.

The introductory article on the subject is

The separate communities, arranged geographically in a circuit of the islands from north to south, are

OUTLINE 6: CENTRAL AMERICA

Marrano Jews came to Mexico with its conquest by the Spaniards, but these groups gradually were merged into the population. It was not until the last quarter of the 19th century that professing Jews began to settle in Central American countries. Since 1933 they have received groups of German Jewish refugees.

A general introduction to the subject is given in

and an account of the settlement of the Jews in American Continent 1:228-30, 234

The individual countries, in geographical order, are

OUTLINE 7: SOUTH AMERICA

The Jewish settlement in South America preceded that in North America, for Marrano Jews came to the former continent soon after its discovery, especially to Brazil. Most of the early settlements disappeared; but Surinam, where the Jews were granted toleration by the Dutch, presents the oldest Jewish community in America. In the latter part of the 19th century a new stream of Jewish immigration into South America began; large communities arose in Argentina and Brazil, and smaller ones in the other countries.

A general introduction to the subject is given in

SOUTH AMERICA 9:665-66

and an account of the settlement of the Jews in

American Continent 1:228-30, 234

The individual countries, in geographical order, are

OUTLINE 8: THE BRITISH ISLES

The history of the Jews in the British Isles falls into two parts. The first is from the Norman Conquest in 1066 to the Expulsion in 1290, during which time the Jewish communities had only local importance. The second, following the Resettlement in the middle of the 17th century, saw the gradual rise of the Jewish community to world importance. The earliest settlements were in the southeastern part of the British Isles, but with the growth of industry and trade other communities arose further north and west, as well as in Scotland and Ireland.

In this outline the historical articles dealing with the three important divisions of the British Isles are given first, followed by supplementary historical articles, and then by the articles on the communities, arranged in geographical order.

ENGLAND 4:110-30 (illus. 9:376)

Southeastern England

Southwestern England

Central England and Wales

Northern England

SCOTLAND 9:446-47

IRELAND 5:585-86

OUTLINE 9: FRANCE

Jews settled in France during the period of the Roman Empire. The first settlements were along the southeastern coast, and it was there that the Jews developed a great cultural center in the Middle Ages, which was annihilated by the expulsions of the 14th and 15th centuries. In the 17th century France acquired new Jewish subjects through its conquest of Alsace. It was the first European country to emancipate the Jews, and Jews came to play an important part in French cultural life until the collapse of 1940. The history of the Jews of France is given in two articles

FRANCE 4:367-85

VICHY FRANCE 10:411-12

Supplementary articles on the history of the French Jews are

The following articles arranged geographically, deal with the Jewish communities of France:

Northwestern France

Southwestern France

Central France

Southern France

Eastern France

OUTLINE 10: THE IBERIAN PENINSULA

Jewish settlements in Spain began probably as early as the first centuries of the Christian Era, but it was only after the Mohammedan conquest in the 8th century that a center arose which for 300 years was the acknowledged leader of Judaism. Its principal achievement was the development of Jewish philosophy, and it was noteworthy for the participation of the Jews in all fields of political and cultural life. The communities of Spain and Portugal were annihilated by persecutions and expulsions in the 14th and 15th centuries, but the refugees brought enlightenment to Jews of modern lands.

The articles in this outline are arranged in the order of countries, supplementary historical articles, and communities in geographical sequence.

SPAIN 9:682-90

Northeastern Spain

Central Spain

Southern Spain

PORTUGAL 8:606-7

OUTLINE 11: GERMANY

The earliest Jewish settlements in Germany were in the Roman cities along the line of the Rhine and the Danube. The communities flourished as centers of trade until the end of the 11th century, when the onslaughts of the Crusaders seriously shook the position of the Jews, and forced them to seek the protection of the emperors. From that time on their situation began to deteriorate, and in the 14th to the 16th centuries community after community was wiped out by massacre or expulsion. Jewish life survived under the protection of the princes, and revived at the beginning of modern times with the coming of Jewish immigrants from the east. In the 19th and 20th centuries the Jewish communities were centers of Jewish learning, and the Jews participated fruitfully in German life and culture, only to suffer almost complete annihilation with the triumph of anti-Semitism in 1933.

The comprehensive article on the subject is

GERMANY 4:541-84

Supplementary articles are

The states and communities of Jewish settlement, arranged in geographical order, are:

Provinces West of the Rhine

The Rhineland

Northern Germany

Oldenburg 8:294-95
Hamburg 5:192-96
  (illus. 3:76; 4:98;
  5:299; 7:41, 476)
Mecklenburg 7:430

Hanover 5:206-8
  Hildesheim 5:358
  Goslar 5:67-68
  Brunswick 2:567-68

Central Germany

Westphalia 10:509
Hesse 5:345-48
  (illus. 2:110)
Cassel 3:57
Fulda 4:469
Saxony 9:386-87
Halberstadt
  5:176-77

Magdeburg 7:269-71
Halle 5:183
Erfurt 4:152
Leipzig 6:601-2
Dresden 3:595-96
Anhalt 1:319

Southern Germany

Baden 2:24
  Mannheim 7:330-32
  Heidelberg 5:291-92
  Karlsruhe 6:322-24
Württemberg 10:580
  Heilbronn 5:294
  Stuttgart 10:91
Bavaria 2:116-20
  (illus. 1:194, 477;
  2:111)
  Würzburg 10:580-81

Bayreuth 2:122
Rothenburg 9:234
Fürth 4:483-84
Nuremberg 8:257-58
  ((illus. 1:351;
  10:123)
Sulzbach 10:97-98
Regensburg 9:111-12
Augsburg 1:613-14
Munich 8:35-36
Passau 8:408

Eastern Germany

Brandenburg
  2:499-500
Prussia 9:12-15
  Jews' Porcelain
  6:149-50
  Berlin 2:206-15
  (illus. 1:113,
  363, 367; 3:77;
  5:405; 8:19)

Frankfort on Oder
  4:406-7
East Prussia
  Danzig 3:468-69
  Königsberg 6:446-47
Silesia 9:534-35
  Breslau 2:521-22
  Dyhernfurth 3:617

ITALY 5:625-39

There is a supplementary article on Mussolini, Benito 8:68-69.

Articles dealing with individual communities, arranged in geographical order, are:

Northern Italy

Barco 2:83
Milan 7:558
Turin 10:325
Cremona 3:408
Mantua 7:334-35
Verona 10:409
Padua 8:342-43
  (illus. 1:195,
  476, 477)
Venice 10:401-4
  (illus. 4:599)

Trieste 10:307-8
Fiume 4:321-22
Genoa 4:533
Parma 8:402-3
Modena 7:606
Ferrara 4:279-80
Reggio nell'Emilia
  9:112
Bologna 2:447
Lugo 7:232-33
Ravenna 9:86

Central Italy

Livorno (Leghorn)
  7:147-49
Pisa 8:542
Lucca 7:227-28
Florence 4:341-43
  (illus. 4:599)
Siena 9:530-31
Urbino 10:380

Pesaro 8:468-69
Fano 4:245
Ancona 1:299-300
Recanati 9:93
Rome 9:187-93 (Titus,
  Arch of 10:257-58;
  illus. 1:292; 4:597)

Southern Italy

Apulia 1:436
Trani 10:291
Bari 2:84
Otranto 8:335

Benevento 2:172
Capua 3:36
Naples 8:99-100
Reggio di Calabria 9:112

Sicily 9:526
Agrigentum 1:128

Sardinia 9:369-70
Cagliari 2:624

Malta 7:305-7

Rhodes 9:153-54

OUTLINE 12: ITALY AND MALTA

Jews settled in southern Italy, Sicily and Malta in the period of the Roman Empire, and the community of Rome was already considerable in the first centuries of the Christian Era. The fate of the Jews in Italy varied greatly in accordance with that of the petty states into which Italy was divided. The communities were never large; nevertheless, they were noteworthy for producing much of the earliest printed Hebrew literature, contributed to the beginnings of modern Hebrew literature and of the Science of Judaism, and their members adopted modern ways of life at an early period. In the 19th century Jews played an important part in the revival of the Italian nation.

The comprehensive article on the subject is

OUTLINE 13: SMALLER COUNTRIES OF NORTHERN EUROPE

Jews did not settle in the countries in Northern Europe until comparatively recent times. The exceptions were Lithuania, which, as part of the Kingdom of Poland, shared the fame of that country as the chief Jewish center from the 15th to the 17th centuries, and Holland, the country which, at the end of the 16th century, was the first to grant Jews full religious toleration. The status of the Jews in the various countries varied with the degrees of freedom enjoyed by the inhabitants; in the 19th and 20th centuries the Jews of the countries along the North Sea and on the Scandinavian Peninsula made notable scientific and cultural contributions. The articles in this outline are arranged by country and communities in geographical sequence, as follows:

OUTLINE 14: POLAND

Jews began to settle in Poland about 1100, from which time on there was a constant stream of immigration from Germany. The situation of the Jews in the country was unusual in that they alone formed the middle class between the nobility and the peasants. In the 15th to the 17th centuries Poland became the most important Jewish center in the world, but after that the situation of the Jews deteriorated with the collapse of the Polish kingdom, and in modern times the Polish Jews have suffered tremendous blows under the reign of anti-Semitism.

The main article on the subject is

The chief Jewish communities of Poland, arranged in geographical order, are:

OUTLINE 15: SMALLER COUNTRIES OF CENTRAL EUROPE

The history of the Jews in the smaller countries is extremely varied, and the local history unusually rich and colorful. A feature of this area is the Danube valley, where Jews began to settle as early as the first centuries of the Christian Era, and where they developed communities which were noted for their learning and for the number of their members who were called to service under the rulers. In modern times many Jews contributed to the progress and culture of their native countries until (with the exception of the Swiss refuge) all the countries were overwhelmed by the flood of anti-Semitism.

The countries follow in geographical sequence from west to east, in each case followed by any additional articles on important rulers and by the communities grouped according to locality.

See also the outline on the BALKAN STATES, under the subheading Roumania, for other cities formerly part of Hungary.

OUTLINE 16: THE BALKAN STATES

Jewish settlements in the Balkan states are very old, for Jews had migrated to Greece as early as the period of the Second Temple and had followed the spread of Roman rule along the eastern coast of the Adriatic Sea in the first centuries of the Christian Era. From the 14th to 18th centuries most of this area was under Turkish rule and the Jews received fairly favorable treatment. Under the modern states the status of the Jews has varied from complete equality to oppressive restrictions.

Each country is given separately, followed by its communities in geographical arrangement.

YUGOSLAVIA 10:617-21

Belgrade 2:150-51	Bosnia 2:479-80
Novi Sad 8:247	Sarajevo 9:367-68
Zagreb 10:625-26	Bitolj 2:386
Spalato 9:690	
(illus 4:599)	

ROUMANIA 9:247-65
Old Roumania

Bucharest 2:571-72	Botoshani 2:484
Jassy 6:43-44	Ploesti 8:552-53

Transylvania and Banat
(formerly part of Hungary)

Temesvár 10:192	Beius 2:142-43
Borsa 2:478	Brasov 2:504-5
Lugoj 7:233	

Bucovina 2:573-74

Czernowitz 3:443	Sadagora 9:307-8
Tighina 10:249	

Bessarabia 2:244-48
Kishinev 6:403-4

BULGARIA 2:584-87

Oescus 8:284	Sofia 9:588-89

ALBANIA 1:156-57
GREECE 5:91-93

Athens 1:580	Aegean Islands 1:104
Corinth 3:369-70	Corfu 3:368-69
Delphi 3:519-20	Salonika 9:327-29
Delos 3:519	Janina 6:36
Crete 3:410-12	

OUTLINE 17: RUSSIA

The history of the Jews in Russia begins as late as 1772, when that country, which had hitherto barred them from its borders, suddenly acquired many thousands of Jewish subjects by the first partition of Poland. From that time on their history is a constant series of restrictions and oppressions, with a few minor alleviations for short periods. Then, in 1917, comes a sudden change: the Jews emerge from medieval ostracism to full equality. Yet their religious and economic position suffers severely from the social revolution; it is only gradually, in the course of years, that Jews begin to find their place in the New Russia and to contribute to its power and progress.

The period prior to 1917 is treated in the articles

RUSSIA 9:278-86

Catherine II 3:67	Cantonists 3:16-17
Alexander I 1:168-69	Alexander II 1:169-70
Nicholas I 8:216	Alexander III 1:170-71
Pale of Settlement	Nicholas II 8:216-17
8:346	

The period after 1917 is described in

SOVIET RUSSIA 9:670-84

The Russian Jewish communities, in geographical arrangement, are:

White Russia 10:511

Minsk 7:576-77	Mohilev 7:610
Homel 5:448	

(see also the frontispiece of volume 4)

Ukraine 10:334-39 (illus. 1:257)

Kiev 6:381-83	Chernigov 3:132
Kharkov 6:375	Dnepropetrovsk 3:581
Odessa 8:282-83	Kamenets Podolsk
Berdichev 2:193-94	6:301-2
Kirovo 6:398	Bar 2:69-70
Balta 2:51-53	Bratzlav 2:505

Bessarabia 2:244-48
Kishinev 6:403-4

Great Russia

Moscow 7:658-59	Belaya Tserkov 2:147
Leningrad 6:606-7	

Crimea 3:412-16

Chufut-Kale 3:194	Karasubazar 6:319
Eupatoria 4:193	Sevastopol 9:485-86
Feodosiya 4:275-76	Kerch 6:363

Caucasus 3:68-69

Baku 2:40	Kherson 6:378

For Jewish agricultural colonies in European Russia, see Colonies, Agricultural 3:288-93.

See also the outline on POLAND. For Siberia, see the outline on CENTRAL ASIA.

OUTLINE 18: AFRICA

The connection of the Jews with Africa begins with the sojourn of the Israelites in Egypt. New settlements arose after the destruction of the First Temple (6th century B.C.E.) and in the Greek period. By the first centuries of the Christian Era Jews were settled all along the northern coast of Africa, where they later prospered in the Middle Ages under Mohammedan rule. It was not until the 19th century that Jews came with other European emigrants to help open up the central and southern parts of the continent. They played an especially important role in the exploration and development of South Africa.

The following articles, arranged geographically, deal with the various African countries and communities:

Barbary States 2:81 (illus. 3:70)

MOROCCO 7:651-53 (illus. 3:76; 4:602)

Daggatuns 3:446	Fez 4:285-86
Casablanca 3:55	

ALGERIA 1:180-82

Oran 8:317-18 (illus. 10:122)
Algiers 1:182-83 (illus. 5:592)
Constantine 3:338

TUNIS AND TUNISIA 10:323-24 (illus. 3:76)

Carthage 2:52-53   Jerba 6:58
Kairwan 6:292

LIBYA 7:44-46

Tripoli 10:309-10   Benghazi 2:173
Cyrene 3:438

EGYPT 4:5-16

Heliopolis 5:305-6   Alexandria 1:176
Red Sea 9:96-97   Cairo 2:626-29
Elephantine 4:64-65

ETHIOPIA 4:182-85

Falashas 4:234-36

BELGIAN CONGO 2:148

KENYA 6:363

ANGOLA 1:318-19

SOUTH AFRICA 9:655-65

Cape Province 3:19-21   Kimberley 6:383
Cape Town 3:21-24   Bloemfontein 2:404-5
Port Elizabeth   Johannesburg 6:166-68
8:602-3   Natal 8:104

MADAGASCAR 7:267

OUTLINE 19: PALESTINE

Palestine is a country that holds widespread interest for many reasons. It was the scene of the passing to and fro of numerous civilizations, and was the cradle of the Jewish people. It is the Holy Land of three religions: Judaism, Christianity and Islam; the adherents of the latter two waged many bloody wars to gain possession of it. In modern times it became, first, a center for Jewish mystics and then, a visioned homeland for the Zionists. Its history presents the story of more than 3,000 years of Jewish settlement.

The general article on the subject is

PALESTINE 8:347-73 (illus. 9:441; 10:121)

The original land conquered by the Israelites is discussed in

Canaan 2:651

The ancient endeavors to supply the country with badly needed water are described in

Aqueducts in Palestine 1:437

The modern status of Palestine is especially treated under

Balfour Declaration 2:45-49
Palestine Mandate 8:376-78

The animals and plants of Palestine are enumerated in

Fauna of Palestine 4:256-63
Flora of Palestine 4:331-41

Modern agrarian laws in Palestine are detailed in

Agriculture 1:127-28

Modern Jewish efforts to develop the country are described in

Colonies, Agricultural 3:268-88 (illus. 3:363)
Halutzim 5:188-90
Palestine Foundation Fund 8:375-76
Jewish National Fund 6:134-38
Hadassah 5:147-50
Palestine Economic Corporation 8:374-75

The following organizations direct their efforts to the support of Palestine and its institutions:

American Jewish Physicians' Committee 1:256
American Zion Commonwealth 1:273
Halukkah 5:188
National Labor Committee for Palestine 8:123-24
United Palestine Appeal 10:348-49

An organization which promoted commercial relations between Palestine and Poland was the Izba Handlowo-Przemyslowa Polsko-Palestynska 5:645

The representative assembly of the Jews of Palestine is

Vaad Leumi 10:388

The vexed problem of the holy places in Palestine is discussed in

Holy Places in Palestine 5:446-47
Machpelah 7:264
Rachel, Tomb of 9:64
Wailing Wall 10:441-42.

The following are the chief geographical divisions of Palestine and the nearby regions, with the cities, rivers, mountains or special features pertaining to them. No attempt has been made to arrange these latter geographically, as their location is often uncertain. An asterisk indicates that the place so marked is mentioned in the Bible or was in existence in Bible times.

1. Phoenicia

*Byblos 2:612-13   *Tyre 10:332
*Sidon 9:528   *Zarephath 10:629

2. The Coastal Plain

*Acco 1:70   *Lydda 7:252
*Aphek 1:414   Ramleh 9:69
*Bene Berak 2:164   *Sharon 9:497
Caesarea (Maritima)   *Shefelah 9:499
  2:623 (illus. 5:325)   Tel-Aviv 10:190-92
Haifa 5:168-71   (illus. 1:514;
*Jabneh 6:1-2   4:337, 341;
*Jaffa 6:26-28   5:342; 9:421)
  (illus. 1:191)

3. Philistia

*Ashdod 1:538	*Gath 4:517
*Ashkelon 1:541	*Gaza 4:518-19
*Ekron 4:42	

4. Galilee 4:500-1 (and neighboring regions)

Arbela 1:454	*Hamath 5:191
*Baalbek 2:5	Jotapata 6:212
(illus 1:210)	*Lebanon 6:580-82
Beth-shearim 2:254	*Luz 7:244
(illus. 3:65)	Meron 7:495
Caesarea (Philippi)	Nazareth 8:134
2:623-24	Pekiin 8:425
Capernaum 3:24	Safed 9:309-11
Gamala 4:505-6	Sepphoris 9:478-79
Gischala 4:614	Usha 10:383

5. The Jezreel Plain

*Jezreel, Plain of	*Gilboa 4:610
6:151-52	*Kishon 6:404
Afule 1:111	*Megiddo 7:437-38
*Carmel 3:48	*Taanach 10:152
*En-dor 4:107	(illus. 1:211)
*En-gannim 4:109	*Tabor 10:155

6. Samaria 9:334-35 (illus. 1:134)

*Beth-el 2:252	*Ramah 9:69
*Ebal 3:619	*Shechem 9:499
*Gerizim 4:541	*Shiloh 9:508
Nablus 8:79	
(illus. 4:541)	

7. *Jerusalem 6:70-80 (illus.1:498;3:75;4:76; 5:148, 284-86, 326, 469; 10:442)

Absalom's Tomb	*Shiloah 9:508
1:56-57	Solomon, Pools of
Acra 1:75	9:637
Antonia 1:412	Tombs of the Kings
Beth-phage 2:253	10:265
*Kidron 6:381	(illus. 1:294)
*Moriah 7:650	*Zion 10:645
*Olives, Mount of	
8:296	

8. Judea 6:251-54

*Ai 1:141	*Gibeon 4:604-5
*Aijalon 1:141	*Hebron 5:287
*Beer-sheba 2:136	(illus. 5:589)
*Beth-horon 2:252	Abraham's Oak
*Bethlehem 2:252-53	1:40
*Beth-shemesh 2:254	*Kiriath-jearim
*Beth-zur 2:254	6:396-97
*Eben-ezer 3:619	*Kiriath-sepher 6:397
Eleutheropolis 4:65	*Lachish 6:505
Emmaus 4:100-1	*Mareshah 7:352
*Ephrathah 4:136	*Mizpah or Mizpeh
*Gezer 4:595-96	7:599
*Gibeah 4:604	*Nob 8:228

9. Negeb 8:144 (and neighboring places)

*Elath 4:44	*Kadesh-barnea 6:276
*Ezion-geber 4:226	*Seir 9:462

10. The Jordan Cleft

*Jordan 6:183	*Jericho 6:67-68
*Arabah 1:438	*Merom, Waters of
*Beth-shean 2:253-54	7:495
*Chinnereth 3:159-60	*Sodom and
*Dead Sea 3:502-3	Gomorrah 9:586-87
*En-gedi 4:109	Tiberias 10:248-49
*Gilgal 4:610	(illus. 6:165;
Hippos 5:371	7:287, 444; 10:121)

The territory to the east of the Jordan is known as

Transjordan 10:292

and is divided into

11. Bashan 2:103-4 (and nearby areas)

*Argob 1:472	*Hauran 5:251
Bathyra 2:112	Iturea 5:640
Carnaim 3:49	*Tamar § 4. 10:168
*Edrei 3:628	Yarmuk 10:586
Gadara 4:490	

12. Gilead 4:610

Gerasa 4:539	*Jabesh-gilead 6:1
*Hermon 5:325	*Ramoth-gilead 9:70
*Jabbok 6:1	

13. Ammon 1:276-77

*Rabbah 9:47

14. Moab 7:602-3

*Arnon 1:485	*Nebo 8:137
*Medeba 7:432	*Pisgah 8:542

15. Places of Uncertain Location

*Kadesh and Kedesh 6:276

See also the outlines on BIBLE, ARCHEOLOGY and ZIONISM.

OUTLINE 20: WESTERN ASIA

Western Asia is so close to Palestine that it is not surprising that Jews settled there at a very early period. They were in Syria in the time of the Kings, in Asia Minor in the days of the Second Temple, and in Arabia in the Talmudic Period. It was in the Jewish communities of Asia Minor that Christianity won some of its first adherents, and in those of Arabia that Mohammed learned monotheism. The once prosperous communities suffered in the course of the centuries from persecution, wars and misgovernment; today only a few remain.

The articles dealing with the countries and communities, in a geographical arrangement, are:

TURKEY 10:326-29

Byzantine Empire	Brusa 2:568
2:613-14	Smyrna 9:576
Adrianople 1:101-2	Ephesus 4:134
Istanbul 5:623-25	

CYPRUS 3:437-38

SYRIA 10:134-36

PETRA 8:471-72

ARABIA 1:438-41

ARMENIA 1:482-83

OUTLINE 21: CENTRAL ASIA

The settlement of the Jews in Central Asia begins with the deportation of the Israelites by the Assyrians and Babylonians in the 8th and 6th centuries B.C.E. Eventually Mesopotamia became a Jewish center of such importance that it furnished the leadership for Jewry from the 5th to the 10th century. From Mesopotamia Jews found their way to Persia, India and other parts of Central Asia. Siberia, however, received its Jewish immigrants from Russia.

The various countries and communities, arranged geographically, are:

IRAQ 5:585

PERSIA 8:460-66

BOKHARA 2:443-44

TURKESTAN 10:325-26

AFGHANISTAN 1:106

INDIA 5:553-57

BURMA 2:605-6

SIBERIA 9:524-25

OUTLINE 22: THE FAR EAST

The oldest Jewish settlements in the Far East were in China, where a small group of Jewish immigrants from Central Asia settled in the Middle Ages and were unknown to the Western world until the 17th century. Other Jewish communities are very recent; they have sprung up in various cities either in the course of the spread of commerce or through the arrival of refugees from European upheavals.

The following are the countries and communities, in geographical order:

CHINA 3:156-59

JAPAN 6:38-40

PHILIPPINE ISLANDS 8:486-87

SINGAPORE 9:554

NETHERLANDS EAST INDIES 8:151-52

AUSTRALIA 1:617-22

TASMANIA 10:177

NEW ZEALAND 8:205

OUTLINE 23: HISTORIANS OF THE JEWS

The writing of Jewish history began with the Bible, the pages of which contain historical writing which measures up to a high standard. In the post-Biblical period there were but few Jewish historians and chroniclers. In modern times the writing of Jewish history revived with the inauguration of the Science of Judaism in the first quarter of the 19th century; since that time numerous Jewish historians have made their contributions to the compilation and interpretation of the past of the Jews.

The main article on the subject is

HISTORIOGRAPHY 5:386-98

Other articles on history and historians may be grouped as follows:

a. Sources
Antiochus, Scroll of 1:340
Seder Olam 9:456-57
Megillath Taanith 7:441
Memorbuch 7:461
Documents, Historical 3:582-83
Archives, Communal 1:467-69
Genizah 4:531-33

b. Ancient Jewish Historians
Jason of Cyrene 6:42 (Northern Africa)
Josephus, Flavius 6:197-202 (P, Rome)
Justus of Tiberias 6:272 (P, Rome)

c. Medieval Historians
Hegesippus 5:291
Josippon 6:210-11
Sherira Gaon 9:504 (Babylonia)
Ahimaaz ben Paltiel 1:139-40 (I)
Ibn Verga, Judah 5:531 (S, Pt)
Ibn Verga, Solomon 5:531 (S, Pt, T)
Joseph ben Joshua Hakohen 6:191 (I)
Gans, David 4:511 (G)

d. Modern Historians
Graetz, Heinrich 5:80-81 (G)
Aronius, Julius 1:487 (G)
Baer, Fritz 2:29 (G, P)
Wolf, Lucien 10:553-54 (E)
Roth, Cecil 9:231-32 (E)
Güdemann, Moritz 5:115-16 (G, A)
Krauss, Samuel 6:467-68 (Hu, A, E)
Rosanes, Solomon A. 9:200-1 (Bu)
Dubnow, Simon 3:606-7 (Ru)
Wiernik, Peter 10:516 (US)
Baron, Salo 2:91 (Po, A, US)
Jacobs, Joseph 6:17-18 (E, US)
Deutsch, Gotthard 3:553-54 (US)
Goodman, Paul 5:59 (E)
Kayserling, Moritz 6:349-50 (G, Swi, Hu)
Klausner, Joseph 6:411-12 (Ru, P)
Krochmal, Nachman 6:472-74 (A)
Marcus, Jacob Rader 7:348 (US)
Marx, Alexander 7:388 (US)
Margolis, Max M. 7:354-55 (US)

The following organizations are devoted to the study of Jewish history:
American Jewish Historical Society 1:253
Jewish Historical Society of England 6:131
Yevreiskoye Istoriko-Etnografitshkoyo Obshtshestvo 10:597

NOTE. For abbreviations see page vi.

PART II: LITERATURE

OUTLINE 24:
LANGUAGES OF THE JEWS

In the course of their life in various countries and under the several civilizations which succeeded one another in Asia, Africa and Europe, the Jews used many languages for their speech and their literature. In some periods they adopted the language of their environment; at others they developed dialects of their own, some of which, transplanted to new surroundings, became independent languages.

The comprehensive article on the subject is

VERNACULARS 10:406-9

The following articles deal with languages spoken by Jews and the resulting Jewish literature (an asterisk indicates a separate outline on the subject):

*Hebrew Language 5:276-81
    *Literature, Hebrew 7:87-96
  Aramaic 1:450-51
    Aramaic Literature of the Jews 1:452-53
  Judeo-Greek 6:254-55
  Judeo-Persian 6:256
    Literature, Judeo-Persian 7:96-98
  Arabian Language 1:442
    Arabic Literature of the Jews 1:442-43
  Judeo-Italian 6:255-56
  Judeo-Spanish 6:257-58
    Literature, Judeo-Spanish 7:98-100
  Yiddish 10:598-602
    *Literature, Yiddish 7:125-35

OUTLINE 25: HEBREW

The knowledge of Hebrew is the key to the understanding of the greater part of Jewish literature. It is the language of the Bible, and hence is studied by both Jews and Christians who desire to grasp the true import of the sacred text. It is the tongue in which much of Jewish literature, as yet untranslated, is written. In modern times, it is the language of the new Palestine and its literature.

The chief article on the subject is

HEBREW LANGUAGE 5:276-81

The following articles deal with the reading and writing of Hebrew:

Alphabet 1:197-205   Accents, Hebrew
Dagesh 3:445-46   1:67-69
Vowels, Hebrew   Abbreviations 1:17
  10:435-36

The study of difficult Hebrew terms, together with the aids to the knowledge of the language, is described in

Hapax Legomena 5:212
Lexicography, Hebrew 7:29-33
Dictionaries, Hebrew 3:562-63
Glossaries 4:621-22
Makre Dardeke 7:300
Aruch 1:516
  Nathan ben Jehiel 8:105-6

Non-Jews who studied the Hebrew language are enumerated in

Hebraists, Christian 5:270-75

The relationship of Hebrew to cognate languages is described in

Semitic Languages and Literature 9:474-76
Aramaic 1:450-51
Arabian Language 1:442

The following organizations are interested in the furtherance of Hebrew as a spoken language:

Histadruth Ivrith 5:385-86
Society of Friends of the Hebrew Language
  9:586
Vaad Halashon 10:387-88

OUTLINE 26: JEWISH LITERATURE

Jewish literature is so varied and written in so many countries and languages that it is extremely difficult to classify in any chronological order. Two classifications are presented, one by language, one by subject matter. An asterisk (*) marks those subjects which are given a special outline of their own.

A. Jewish Literature Classified by Language.

*Literature, Hebrew 7:87-96
  Poetry, Hebrew 8:556-59
*Literature, Yiddish 7:125-35
  Aramaic Literature of the Jews 1:452-53
  Arabic Literature of the Jews 1:442-43
  Literature, Judeo-Spanish 7:98-100
  Literature, Judeo-Persian 7:96-98
  American Literature on and by Jews 1:259-70
  Literature on and by Jews 7:100-25

B. Jewish Literature Classified by Categories (Chronological Order)

*Bible 2:280-84
  *Apocrypha 1:422-24
  *Pseudepigrapha 9:20
Hellenistic Literature,   Lexicography
  for which see   7:29-33
Hellenism 5:306-7   *Bible Exegesis
*Talmud 10:160-65   2:301-6
*Midrash 7:538   Codes 3:230-32

OUTLINE 27:

THE CONTENTS OF THE BIBLE

The Bible is the first great compilation of Jewish literature. The writings contained in it span many centuries: according to tradition, from Moses to Ezra; according to modern scholars, from the period of the Judges to the days of the Maccabees. It is a sacred book for both Jews and Christians, who for centuries have pored over its pages. The first step in the knowledge of the Bible is to become familiar with its contents, guided by the teachings of both ancient interpreters and modern scholarship.

The introductory article on the subject is

BIBLE 2:280-84

The following articles furnish supplementary information:

For the historical background of the Bible, see the outline on JEWISH HISTORY BY PERIODS, sections 1 through 5.

The three main divisions of the Hebrew Bible are

Pentateuch 8:434
(see also Torah § 3. 10:267-68)
Prophets (see 8:658)
Hagiographa 5:164-65

The following articles are arranged for the purpose of the study of the contents of the Bible. Before turning to the text of any book, the student should read the article pertaining to it, by way of introduction. Then the book itself should be read, together with the sub-articles on topics and persons, which have been selected because of their historical, scholarly or traditional interest. (The numbers preceding the articles indicate chapters of the book.)

Genesis 4:528-30

OUTLINE 28: BIBLE INTERPRETATION AND INTERPRETERS

The study of the Bible has been followed by two separate and distinct schools of Jewish and Christian scholarship. The first has attempted to find out the meaning of the accepted text of the Bible; it accepts the traditional authorship and seeks to derive from the text lessons for its own and future generations. The second goes further and attempts to emend the text as well as to assign it to its proper sources, often widely clashing with tradition. Though the two schools are often contemporaneous, their methods and approach are so distinct that they must be treated separately. The first, therefore, is treated as Bible Exegesis; the second, as Bible Criticism.

1. BIBLE EXEGESIS 2:301-6

The most important Jewish Bible exegetes, in chronological order, were:

Special aid to this work of interpreting the Bible has been furnished by

2. BIBLE CRITICISM 2:284-93

The most important of the Bible critics, in chronological order, are

Bible Criticism—*Continued*

Kuenen, Abraham 6:483 (Ho)
Marti, Karl 7:385-86 (G)
Dillmann, August 3:565 (G)
Kautzsch, Emil 6:346 (G)
Kittel, Rudolf 6:408-9 (G)
Bertholet, Alfred 2:242 (G)
Meyer, Eduard 7:514-15 (G)
Nöldeke, Theodor 8:231 (G)
Haupt, Paul 5:251 (US)
Nowack, Wilhelm 8:247 (G)
Moore, George Foote 7:637-38 (US)
Geiger, Abraham 4:521-22 (G)
Buttenwieser, Moses 2:610-11 (US)
Morgenstern, Julian 7:645-46 (US)
Torczyner, Harry 10:277-78 (G, P)
Jastrow, Morris, Jr. 6:45-46 (US)
Bernfeld, Simon 2:227 (G)

The most far-reaching conclusions of Bible Criticism are those that deal with the

Hexateuch 5:352-54

This is analyzed into the following codes, in historical order:

Kenite Document 6:360-61
Book of the Covenant 2:455
Elohist Code 4:89-91
Jahvist Code 6:31-34
Deuteronomic Code 3:549-50
Holiness Code 5:418-21
Priestly Code 8:637-42

The following articles or sections of articles are written from the point of view of the modern critical scholarship of the Bible:

Adam § 1. 1:76-78
Angels § 1. 1:304-10
Ark of the Covenant
  1:478-79
Ark of Noah
  1:479-80
Breastplate 2:516-17
Decalogue 3:506-13
Ehud 4:21
Face of God: 4:231
Flood 4:330-31
Harvest Festivals
  5:235

Isaiah §§ 2. and 3.
  5:604-5
Levites 7:1-4
Priests 8:642-44
Retaliation, Law of
  9:242-44
Tables of the Law
  10:153-54
Universalism and
  Particularism
  10:353-57

OUTLINE 29: BIBLE INFLUENCE ON CIVILIZATION

It has been generally acknowledged that the Bible has had an extraordinary influence upon modern life and civilization, both Jewish and Christian. The chief reason for this influence has been the creation and diffusion of

Bible Translations 2:334-46

Targum 10:173-75
Onkelos 8:301
Septuagint 9:479-81
Aquila 1:437-38
Symmachus 10:119
Theodotion 10:242
Hexapla 5:352
Peshitta 8:469
Vulgate 10:437

This has led to the widespread practice of

Bible Reading 2:333-34

The influence of the Bible in language appears in

Hebraisms 5:270

Its influence in other fields is treated in the articles

Bible in Art 2:306-16
Bible in Drama 2:316-19
Bible in Literature 2:319-26
Bible in Music 2:326-27

For a study of the ideas and movements developed in the Bible, see outlines 37-38, 41-44, 48, 54, 56-60 and 71.

For the important ideals which were transmitted to humanity through the Bible, see the articles

Brotherhood of Man
  2:558-60
Covenant 3:389
Ethics §2. 4:175-78
Fatherhood of God
  4:252-54
God 5:1-2
Holiness § 1. 5:416-18
Inspiration 5:571-75
Justice 6:268-70

Kingdom of Heaven
  6:386-87
Liberty 7:34-36
Messiah 7:499-500
Peace 8:418-19
Prophets and Prophecy
  8:658-64
Social Legislation
  9:579-80
Wisdom 10:536-38

OUTLINE 30:
APOCRYPHA AND PSEUDEPIGRAPHA

The Apocrypha and Pseudepigrapha are a group of Jewish writings which have been preserved almost entirely through Christian piety. Although they were not admitted into the Bible canon, they are in many ways a continuation of Biblical literature. The Apocrypha in particular are a fine source for the study of Judaism in the period between the Bible and the Talmud. The Pseudepigrapha contain noble ethical teachings, but a number of them come from Jewish sects or mystics which had more influence upon Christianity than upon the later development of Judaism.

The articles dealing with this field are

APOCRYPHA 1:422-24

Esdras, Books of 4:163-65
Tobit 10:259 (illus. 1:423; 2:323)
  Ahikar 1:138-39
  Sarah 9:367

Judith 6:264 (illus. 2:325)
   Achior 1:71-72
   Bethulia 2:254
   Holophernes 5:445
Esther § 2b. 4:170
Wisdom of Solomon 10:538-39
Sirach 9:558-59
Baruch 2:95-96
Daniel, Additions to 3:466
Manasseh, Prayer of 7:312
Maccabees, Books of 7:260-64

PSEUDEPIGRAPHA 9:20

Enoch, Book of 4:131-33
Testaments of the Twelve Patriarchs 10:202
Jubilees, Book of 6:218-19
Psalms of Solomon 9:19-20
Moses, Ascension of 8:8-9
Baruch, Apocalypse of 2:96-97
Aristeas, Letter of 1:473
Adam, Books of 1:78-80
Isaiah, Ascension of 5:605-6
Sibylline Books 9:525
Abraham, Apocalypse of 1:38
Abraham, Testament of 1:40
Job, Testament of 6:159
Elijah, Apocalypse of 4:76
Solomon, Testament of 9:637
Zephaniah, Apocalypse of 10:640

OUTLINE 31: THE TALMUD

The Talmud is the second great compilation of Jewish literature. It is the summation of the teachings of the great Jewish leaders from the 2nd century B.C.E. to the end of the 5th century C.E., arranged in the form of a legal code, the Mishnah, and a commentary, the Gemara. The Mishnah is brief, precise and orderly in structure; the Gemara is voluble, argumentative, and digressive, with stories and opinions on almost every conceivable topic. There are two separate Talmuds, one written in Palestine, the other and more important one in Babylonia; each contains a Gemara to about 30 of the 63 tractates of the Mishnah.

The comprehensive article on the subject is

TALMUD 10:160-65

Related articles are
Mishnah 7:581-82
Tosefta 10:283-84
Baraitha 2:76-79
Hermeneutics, Talmudic 5:323-24

The Talmud consists of a number of tractates, arranged into six divisions, as follows:

1. Zeraim 10:640

Berachoth 2:190-91	Maaseroth 7:258
Peah 8:421	Maaser Sheni 7:258
Demai 3:520	Hallah § 2. 5:183
Kilayim 6:383	Orlah 8:324
Shebiith 9:498-99	Bikkurim 2:351-52
Terumoth 10:201	

2. Moed 7:608

Sabbath 9:299-300	Betzah 2:273
Erubin 4:159-60	Rosh Hashanah
Pesahim 8:468	9:227-29
Shekalim 9:500	Taanith 10:152
Yoma 10:605	Moed Katan 7:608
Sukkah 10:95	Hagigah § 2. 5:164

3. Nashim 8:102

Yebamoth 10:587	Sotah 9:653
Kethuboth 6:373	Gittin 4:614-16
Nedarim 8:141	Kiddushin 6:381
Nazir 8:134-35	

4. Nezikin 8:216

Baba (3 tractates)	Eduyoth 4:1
2:7-8	Abodah Zarah 1:30-31
Sanhedrin 9:363	Aboth 1:32-33
Makkoth 7:299	Horayoth 5:453
Shebuoth 9:499	

5. Kodashim 6:425

Zebahim 10:631	Kerithoth 6:364
Menahoth 7:467	Meilah 7:443
Hullin 5:480-81	Tamid 10:168
Bechoroth 2:127-28	Middoth 7:537
Arachin 1:446	Kinnim 6:395-96
Temurah 10:197	

6. Toharoth 10:260

Kelim 6:357	Niddah 8:217
Ohaloth 8:287	Machshirin 7:264-65
Negaim 8:144	Zabim 10:622
Parah 8:389-90	Tebul Yom 10:187
Toharoth 10:260	Yadayim 10:583
Mikvaoth 7:557	Uktzin 10:339-40

In addition, there are the seven
Talmud Tractates, Minor 10:167-68

Sefer Torah 9:459	Abadim 1:12
Mezuzah 7:527	Kuthim 6:493
Tefillin 10:187	Gerim 4:540
Tzitzith 10:333	

and six others usually included in editions of the Talmud:

Aboth de Rabbi Nathan 1:34
Soferim 9:587-88
Semahoth 9:472
Kallah 6:297
Derech Eretz Rabbah 3:540
Derech Eretz Zuta 3:540

24—LITERATURE

The following is a list of the chief teachers whose words are recorded in the Talmud:

1. The Chain of Tradition

Synagogue, The Great 10:132
Soferim 9:587
Simon the Just 9:543
Antigonus of Socho 1:336
Zugoth 10:675
Jose ben Joezer of Zeredah 6:183-84
Jose ben Johanan of Jerusalem 6:184
Joshua ben Perahiah 6:209
Nittai (Mattai) of Arbela 8:224
Judah ben Tabbai 6:225
Simeon ben Shetah 9:540-41
Shemaiah 9:502
Abtalion 1:59-60
Hillel I 5:362-63 (illus. 1:215)
Shammai 9:495

2. Tannaim 10:170-71

First Generation
Beth Hillel and Beth Shammai 2:251-52
Akabiah ben Mahalalel 1:142
Gamaliel I 4:506
Simeon ben Gamaliel I 9:540
Johanan ben Zakkai 6:164-66
Bathyra (family) 2:112
Eleazar ben Zadok § 1. 4:63
Jonathan ben Uzziel 6:182

Second Generation
Gamaliel II 4:506-7
Eliezer ben Hyrcanus 4:69-70
Joshua ben Hananiah 6:207-8
Eleazar ben Azariah 4:61
Eleazar ben Arach 4:60-61
Nahum of Gimzo 8:89
Zadok 10:625
Eliezer ben Jacob § 1. 4:70
Hanina ben Dosa 5:205
Dosa ben Harchinas 3:590-91
Eleazar of Modin 4:63-64
Halafta 5:175

Third Generation
Tarfon 10:172-73
Ishmael ben Elisha 5:608-9
Akiba ben Joseph 1:144-50
Hananiah ben Teradyon 5:201
Johanan ben Nuri 6:164
Jose Hagelili 6:184
Elisha ben Abuyah 4:80-81
Judah ben Baba 6:223
Ben Zoma 2:161
Ben Azzai, Simeon 2:157-58
Eleazar ben Zadok § 2. 4:63
Eliezer ben Judah 4:70

Fourth Generation
Meir 7:443-44
Judah ben Ilai 6:223-24
Jose ben Halafta 6:183
Simeon ben Yohai 9:541

Eleazar ben Shammua 4:62
Johanan Hasandelar 6:166
Simeon ben Gamaliel II 9:540
Phinehas ben Jair 8:516
Eleazar Hisma 4:63
Eliezer ben Jacob § 2. 4:70
Jonathan 6:180-81
Josiah 6:210
Nehemiah 8:148

Fifth Generation
Judah Hanasi 6:229-30
Nathan the Babylonian 8:105
Eleazar ben Simeon 4:62
Simeon ben Eleazar 9:539
Bar Kappara 2:70-72
Eleazar ben Zadok § 3. 4:63

Sixth Generation
Bannaah 2:64
Hiyya bar Abba § 1. 5:404
Abba Aricha (Rab) 1:14-15

Uncertain Period
Ben Bag Bag and Ben He He 2:158
Eleazar Hakappar 4:63

3. Amoraim 1:277-78

First Palestinian Generation
Hanina bar Hama 5:205
Jannai 6:36-37
Hoshaiah Rabbah 5:464-65
Judah Nesiah § 1. 6:230
Joshua ben Levi 6:208-9
Kahana § 1. 6:283

First Babylonian Generation
Mar Samuel 7:344-45
Abba Aricha (Rab) 1:14-15

Second Palestinian Generation
Johanan bar Nappaha 6:164
Simeon ben Lakish 9:540
Isaac ben Eleazar 5:590
Simlai 9:542

Second Babylonian Generation
Huna 5:482
Judah bar Ezekiel 6:222
Kahana § 2. 6:283

Third Palestinian Generation
Isaac Nappaha 5:592
Eleazar ben Pedath 4:62
Abbahu 1:16
Ammi 1:276
Assi 1:555
Judah Nesiah § 2. 6:230
Hiyya bar Abba § 2. 5:404
Levi 6:621

Third Babylonian Generation
Hamnuna 5:200
Sheshet 9:504
Rabbah bar Huna 9:47
Rabbah bar Hana 9:47
Rabbah bar Nahmani 9:48
Amram Hasida 1:283

Fourth Palestinian Generation
Dimi 3:566

Fourth Babylonian Generation
Abaye 1:12-13   Nahman bar Isaac
Raba 9:47   8:86

Fifth Palestinian Generation
Berechiah 2:194
Tanhuma bar Abba 10:170
Hillel II 5:363

Fifth Babylonian Generation
Kahana § 3. 6:283-84

Sixth Babylonian Generation
Amemar of Nehardea   Ashi 1:541
1:223   Mar Zutra I 7:345

4. Saboraim 9:301-2

The study of the Talmud is treated in the following articles:

Talmud   Rashi 9:78-79
   Commentaries   Tosafoth 10:282
   10:166-67   Yeshiva 10:592-95

OUTLINE 32: MIDRASH

The general article on this subject is

MIDRASH 7:538

Midrash is of two types, Halachic and Haggadic. To understand the meaning of these terms, one should read the articles
Halachah 5:172-75   Haggadah 5:155-56

A. The Halachic Midrash Compilations
Mechilta 7:429
Mechilta Lesefer Debarim 7:429
Mechilta of Rabbi Simeon ben Yohai 7:429
Sifra 9:531
Sifre 9:531
Sifre Zuta 9:531

B. The Haggadic Midrash Compilations
1. Midrash Rabbah 7:540-41
Midrash Genesis 7:539
Midrash Exodus 7:539
Midrash Leviticus 7:540
Midrash Numbers 7:540
Midrash Deuteronomy 7:538-39
Midrash Song of Songs 7:541
Midrash Ruth 7:541
Midrash Lamentations 7:540
Midrash Ecclesiastes 7:539
Midrash Esther 7:539

2. Other Midrash Compilations to Biblical Books
Midrash Hagadol 7:539-40
Midrash Samuel 7:541
Midrash Psalms 7:540
Midrash Proverbs 7:540

3. General Midrash Compilations
Tanhuma 10:169-70   Midrash Galuth 7:539
Pesikta 8:469-70   Akiba, Alphabet of 1:144
Midrashim, Minor   Sefer Hatagin 9:459
   7:541   En Yaakob 4:102-3
Tanna Debe Eliyahu   Yalkut 10:586
   10:170   Yalkut Shimeoni 10:586
Pirke de Rabbi Eliezer
   8:541

4. Articles or Sections of Articles Devoted to Midrashic Expositions
Aaron § 2. 1:1-2   Elijah § 2. 4:75
Abraham § 2. 1:36-37   Eve § 2. 4:198
Absalom § 2. 1:56   Isaac § 2. 5:588-89
Adam § 2. 1:78   Jacob §2. 6:8
Asenath 1:536-37   Jeremiah § 4. 6:66-67
Athenians in Talmud   Jerusalem § III. 6:78-80
   and Midrash 1:579-80   Joseph § 2. 6:188
Balaam § 2. 2:42   Moses §2. 8:6-8
Cain and Abel § 2.   Sheba, Queen of § 2.
   2:626   9:498
Creation § 3. 3:396   Temple in Talmud and
David § 2. 3:482-83   Midrash 10:196-97
Egypt § III. 4:11-12

OUTLINE 33: HEBREW LITERATURE

The chief article on the subject is

LITERATURE, HEBREW 7:87-96

Since Hebrew literature up to modern times comprises practically all the authoritative literature on various Jewish subjects, the most important works are treated under a variety of headings, such as LITERATURE, BIBLE, TALMUD, MIDRASH, JEWISH PHILOSOPHY, LITURGY, JEWISH LAW, ETHICS, SYNAGOGUE and EDUCATION. The following are the most important modern Hebrew authors, arranged in chronological order:

Luzzatto, Moses Hayim 7:246-47 (I, Ho)
Meassefim 7:428 (G)
Erter, Isaac 4:157-58 (A)
Perl, Josef 8:458 (A)
Lebensohn, Abraham Dob Hacohen 6:582-83 (Ru)
Lebensohn, Micah Joseph 6:583-84 (Ru)
Mapu, Abraham 7:343-44 (Ru)
Abramowitsch, Shalom Jacob 1:49-51 (Ru)
Braudes, Reuben Asher 2:506 (Ru, A, Ro)
Brandstaetter, Mordecai David 2:503 (A)
Gordon, Judah Loeb 5:63-65 (Ru)
Gottlober, Abraham Bär 5:72 (Ru)
Lilienblum, Moses Leib 7:61-62 (Ru)
Lewin, Judah Löb 7:22 (Ru)
Smolenskin, Peretz 9:573-75 (Ru, A)
Manne, Mordecai Zebi 7:328-29 (Ru)
Dolicki, Menahem Mendel 3:587 (Ru, US)
Schapira, Constantin Abba 9:389 (Ru)

Ahad Haam 1:135-36 (Ru, Po, P)
Feierberg, Mordecai Zeeb 4:266 (Ru)
Peretz, Isaac Loeb 8:436-37 (Po)
Steinberg, Judah 10:43-44 (Ro, Ru)
Bialik, Hayim Nahman 2:276-78 (Ru, P)
Tschernikowski, Saul 10:318-20 (Ru)
Cohen, Jacob 3:246-47 (Po, P)
Shneur, Zalman 9:512-13 (Ru, F, US)
Shimonowitz, David 9:508-9 (P)
Brenner, Joseph Hayim 2:518-19 (Ru, P)
Berdyczewski, Micah Joseph 2:194 (Ru, G)
Agnon, Samuel Joseph 1:119 (A, G, P)
Smilansky, Moses 9:572 (P)
Frischman, David 4:462-63 (Ru)
Brainin, Reuben 2:493 (Ru, A, G, US)

OUTLINE 34: YIDDISH LITERATURE

The comprehensive article on the subject is

LITERATURE, YIDDISH 7:125-35

The following are the most important Yiddish writers of modern times, arranged in chronological order:

Levin, Mendel 6:631 (Po, A)
Axenfeld, Israel 1:650 (Ru)
Levinsohn, Isaac Baer 6:634-35 (Ru, A)
Ettinger, Solomon 4:190-91 (Po)
Dick, Eisik Meir 3:560-61 (Ru)
Abramowitsch, Shalom Jacob 1:49-51 (Ru)
Peretz, Isaac Loeb 8:436-37 (Po)
Sholom Aleichem 9:516-18 (Ru, US)
Rosenfeld, Morris 9:213-14 (Ru, E, US)
Frug, Simon Samuel 4:466-67 (Ru)
Bloomgarden, Solomon 2:413-14 (Ru, US)
Goldfaden, Abraham 5:20-21 (Ru, A, Ro, US)
Reisen, Abraham 9:121 (Ru, US)
Spector, Mordecai 9:691-92 (Ru, US)
Rapoport, Solomon 9:75 (A)
Asch, Sholom 1:533-34 (Po, F, Swi, US)
Frischman, David 4:462-63 (Ru)
Gordin, Jacob 5:60 (Ru, US)
Pinski, David 8:538-39 (Ru, US)
Hirschbein, Peretz 5:380 (Ru, US)
Cahan, Abraham 2:624 (US)
Niger, Samuel 8:219-21 (Ru, US)
Nadir, Moishe 8:82 (US)
Halper, Leivick 5:186 (Ru, US)
Kahanovitsch, Pinkhos 6:284 (Ru)
Opatoshu, Joseph 8:302-3 (Ru, US)
Litwakov, Moses 7:145 (Ru)
Reisen, Zalman 9:122 (Ru, Po)
Singer, Israel Joshua 9:555-56 (Po, US)
Markish, Peretz 7:359 (Ru)
Kulbak, Moses 6:485-86 (Ru)
Kushnirov, Aaron 6:493 (Ru)

OUTLINE 35:

BOOKS AND MANUSCRIPTS

This outline is concerned entirely with the physical makeup of Jewish books and those who took an interest in their manufacture and collection. The contents of the books are presented in various other outlines that treat of Jewish literature, such as Bible, Talmud, Literature, Hebrew Literature and Yiddish Literature.

The general article on the subject is

BOOKS 2:458-70

The earliest Jewish books were naturally in the form of

Manuscripts 7:336-42

Related topics are
    Writing 10:578-79
    Notarikon 8:246
    Calligraphy 2:647
    Illumination of Manuscripts 5:539-42

Of special interest in this connection are the following types of manuscripts:
    Bible Manuscripts 2:330-33
    Haggadah, Passover § 2. 5:157-64

With the development of Jewish literature, books began to acquire such special features as
    Titles of Hebrew Books 10:255-57
    Chronogram 3:192-93
    Haskamah 5:245
With the invention of printing, the manufacture of Hebrew books became the task of
    Printers and Printing 8:645-47
    The earliest of these books are known as

Incunabula 5:548-53

The earliest printers of Jewish books were
    Conat, Abraham ben Solomon 3:324 (I)
    Abraham, the Dyer, of Pesaro 1:43 (I)
    Soncino, Gershom ben Moses 9:647 (I)
    Soncino, Joshua 9:647 (I)
    Gunzenhauser, Azriel Ashkenazi 5:133 (I)
    Abraham ben Garton 1:42 (I)
    Bomberg, Daniel 2:448-50 (I)
    Adelkind 1:84 (I)
    Bragadini 2:491 (I)
    Kohen 6:427 (G)
    Halicz 5:180 (Po)
    Usque, Abraham 10:383-84 (I)
    Foa, Tobiah 4:346 (I)
    Manasseh ben Israel 7:312-13 (Ho)
    Benveniste, Immanuel 2:188-89 (Ho)
    Uri Phoebus ben Aaron Halevi 10:380-81
        (Ho, Po)
    Athias, Joseph 1:580 (Ho)
    Alexander 1:174 (E)
    Bak 2:36 (I)

After this, the work of printing is carried on by
Publishing Houses 9:31-34

The following articles deal with organizations and publishing houses devoted to the issuing of Jewish books:
Achiasaph 1:71
Jewish Publication Society of America 6:138-40
Mekize Nirdamin 7:449
Philo Verlag 8:496-97
Soncino Gesellschaft 9:647
Stybel, Abraham J. 10:91-92

The publication and reading of books was limited by
Books, Prohibited 2:471
Censorship 3:80-83
Index Librorum Prohibitorum 5:553

A special type of books for the masses were the
Chapbooks 3:109-11

Worn out books were often stored in a
Genizah 4:531-33

The most noted collectors of Jewish books were and are
Fano, Menaham Azariah 4:245-46 (I)
Levita, Elijah 6:639-40 (I)
Joseph Nasi 6:192-94 (T)
Benveniste, Samuel 2:189 (S)

Manasseh ben Israel 7:312-13 (Ho)
Montezinos, David 7:632 (Ho)
Oppenheim (Oppenheimer), David 8:304-5 (A)
Rosenthal, Eliezer, described in
Rosenthaliana 9:222 (Ho)
Almanzi, Joseph 1:193 (I)
Merzbacher, Abraham 7:496 (G)
Michael, Heimann Joseph 7:529-30 (G)
Straschun, Mathias 10:73-74 (Vilna)
Simonsen, David 9:549-50 (D)
Kaufmann, David 6:342-43 (Hu)
Gottheil, Gustave 5:70 (US)
Günzburg, Baron David 5:132 (Ru)
Halberstam, Solomon Zalman Hayim 5:177(Po)
Sassoon, David Solomon 9:376 (E)
Adler, Elkan Nathan 1:90 (E)
Rosenbach, Abraham S. Wolf 9:205 (US)

Such collectors, as well as other lovers of Jewish books, often had their individual
Bookplates 2:456-58

The scientific collection and classification of Jewish books is treated in

Libraries, Jewish 7:38-43

Bibliography, Jewish 2:346-48

For the various divisions into which Jewish books are classified, see the LITERATURE outline.

PART III: RELIGION

OUTLINE 36: RELIGION IN GENERAL

Religion arises as a result of the aspiration of man to comprehend the Power that is behind the universe and to adjust his life in accordance with the purposes and will of that Power. Hence every religion contains a group of beliefs, a link between the Deity and the worshipper, and a set of divine commandments that humanity is to follow. The earliest religions were crude, corresponding to the insufficient knowledge of the time; with the increase in human experience and understanding, higher forms developed until ethical monotheism was achieved. In modern times, religion has been subjected to critical study and extensive analysis.

The introductory article on the subject is

RELIGION 9:124-26

The other articles in this field may be grouped as follows:

1. Primitive Forms of Religion

Totemism 10:284	Tree Worship 10:299
Animal Worship 1:319-20	Ancestor Worship 1:298
	Astral Worship 1:569-70
Bull Worship 2:587	Taboo 10:154-55
Calf Worship 2:642	

2. The Achievement of Monotheism

Henotheism 5:315	Dualism 3:604
Syncretism 10:133	Pantheism 8:384
Monotheism 7:623-24	

3. Modern Speculations on Religion

Deism 3:516	Agnosticism 1:119-20
Theism 10:240	Atheism 1:578-79
Skepticism 9:561	

OUTLINE 37: RELIGION OF ISRAEL

Though Judaism in its doctrines reaches back to the earliest period of the history of Israel, it was not until the beginning of the period of the Second Temple that it attained its full formulation. The religion of the Israelites prior to that time is usually treated under the title Religion of Israel. This Religion of Israel inaugurated many of the customs and institutions that survived down to the destruction of the Second Temple in 70 C.E. The chief article on the subject is

RELIGION OF ISRAEL 9:126-28

The features of this religion can be grouped as follows:

1. The Struggle with Idolatry

Idolatry 5:536	Asherah 1:540
Baal § 1. 2:1-2	Tammuz 10:168
Astarte 1:569	

2. Shrines

Matzebah 7:413	Temple 10:193-97
High Place 5:357-58	Holy of Holies 5:446
Altar 1:210-11	

3. Cult Objects

Teraphim 10:199	Urim and Thummim
Breastplate 2:516-17	10:381
Ephod 4:134	

4. Modes of Learning the Will of God

Divination 3:575	Prophets and Prophecy
Augury 1:614-15	8:658-64
Oracle 8:316-17	

5. Consecrated Persons

Priests 8:642-44	Nazirite 8:135

Also a relic of the Baal and Astarte religion
Kedeshah 6:353

6. Mode of Worship

Sacrifice 9:306-7	Purification 9:35-36
First-Fruits 4:313-15	Red Heifer 9:95-96
Showbread 9:519	Incense 5:548

Also a practice inherited from idolatry and eventually abolished
Child Sacrifice 3:152-53

7. Sacred Days

Sabbath 9:295-99	Harvest Festivals
New Moon 8:171	5:235

8. Special Ideas

Sheol 9:503
Universalism and Particularism 10:353-57

For the subsequent religious development, *see* the outline on JUDAISM.

OUTLINE 38: JUDAISM

Judaism is a religion that is more than a set of beliefs; it is a way of life developed as the result of the inspiration of numerous Jewish teachers and embodied in the form of laws. Its doctrines are simple and its creed rational; but its ethical standards and social requirements are most comprehensive and its requirements of the individual follower reach into every part of life. It is therefore presented here in its double form of doctrine and duty.

The comprehensive article on the subject is

JUDAISM 6:232-37

The question of the presence of dogmas in Judaism is discussed in

Dogmas 3:585-86

and attempts at formulating a creed in

Creed 3:400-3

The teachings of Judaism may be grouped as follows:

1. Articles of Faith

God 5:1-4
Man 7:309-11
Fatherhood of God 4:252-54
Brotherhood of Man 2:558-61
Chosen People 3:164-69
Torah 10:267-69
Reward and Punishment 9:150-51
Immortality 5:546-48
Messianic Era 7:503-5

2. Ethical and Social Ideals

Truth 10:317-18
Justice 6:268-70
Righteousness 9:165
Holiness 5:416-18
Liberty 7:34-37
Universalism of Judaism, The 10:357-62

3. Personal Standards of Religious Conduct

Piety 8:530-31
Saints and Saintliness 9:316-17
Spirituality 10:10-13
Wisdom 10:536-38
Optimism and Pessimism 8:315-16
Kavvanah 6:346-48
Kingdom of Heaven 6:386-91
Kiddush Hashem and Hillul Hashem 6:380-81

OUTLINE 39: JEWISH THEOLOGY

Theology is the systematic presentation of religious ideas. It is the process that analyses the fundamental elements of religion, classifies them by subjects, develops them into a coherent system, and answers the various questions that arise in the believer's mind. A general exposition of this subject is given in

THEOLOGY 10:242-44

The theological articles may be grouped around the following heads:

1. The Nature of God

God, Knowledge of 5:4-5
God, Names of 5:6-8
Yahveh 10:584-86 (see also the erroneous Jehovah 6:54-55)
Tetragrammaton 10:203
Ancient of Days 1:299
En Sof 4:102
Attributes of God 1:609-10
Thirteen Attributes 10:245

Anthropomorphism 1:334-35
Heaven 5:269
Seventh Heaven 9:486
Glory of God 4:621
Shekinah 9:501

2. God and the World

Cosmology 3:372
Creation 3:395-98
Demiurge 3:529
Logos 7:167-68
Miracle 7:578-79

3. The Nature of Man

His Physical and Spiritual Being
Life 7:58
Ages of Man 1:117-18
Old Age 8:293-94
Death 3:503-4
Body 2:436-37
Soul 9:653-54

His Choice of Action
Free Will 4:428-31
Evil Inclination 4:200
Fatalism 4:252
Predestination 8:629

His Divine Nature
Image of God 5:542
Son of God 9:646

The Unity of Humanity
Equality 4:148-49

4. God and Man

God's Rule Over Man
Theodicy 10:241-42
Good and Evil 5:55-56

God's Protection and Beneficence
Providence 9:10
Mercy 7:492-93

God's Chastisements
Jealousy § 1. 6:49
Wrath of God 10:577-78
Suffering 10:93

Man's Attitude Toward God
Fear of God 4:264
Love 7:210-11
Dependence 3:539-40
Faith 4:233
Justification 6:270

Problem of Intercession
Mediation and Mediator 7:433-34
Redeemer 9:97-98

The Hope of Man from God
Redemption 9:98
Salvation 9:332-33

5. God and Israel

Theocracy 10:240-41
Mission of Israel 7:582-84
Servant of God 9:484-85
Covenant 3:389

6. Revelation 9:147-48

Theophany 10:244-45
Inspiration 5:571-75
Prophets and Prophecy 8:658-64
Apocalypse 1:416-17
Ruah Hakodesh 9:268
Bath Kol 2:107
Ascension 1:531

7. Sin and Atonement

The Keeping of the Record
Recording Angel 9:95
Book of Life 2:455

Wrongdoing and Its Consequences

Sin 9:552-53   Fall of Man 4:239-41
Abomination 1:31-32   Damnation 3:452-53

The Averters of Punishment

Repentance 9:134-35   Charity 3:113-14
Prayer 8:617-19
Zechuth Aboth 10:633-34 (known also as Merit of the Fathers 7:493 and Original Virtue 8:324)

The Return to God

Atonement 1:601-8   Reconciliation 9:95
Forgiveness 4:357

The doctrines about the events of the future are grouped under the general head of

Eschatology 4:161-63

They fall into the following categories:

8. The Fate of the Soul

Pre-existence 8:629   Abraham's Bosom
Olam Hazeh and   1:38-40
   Olam Haba   Academy on High 1:67
   8:292-93   Paradise 8:387-89
Future Life 4:484-86   Resurrection 9:141-42
Gehinnom 4:520-21   Souls, Transmigration
Purgatory 9:35   of 9:654-55

9. The Fate of the World

Messiah 7:499-503
Judgment, Day of 6:263
Last Judgment 6:544-46
Millennium 7:562

OUTLINE 40: JEWISH PHILOSOPHY

Jewish philosophy is different in nature from general philosophy. General philosophy ignores religion completely, starts with no preconceived ideas, and attempts to build up a conception of the world in accordance with the dictates of reason. Jewish philosophy, however, is actually a phase of Jewish theology. It is the systematic attempt to reconcile the teachings of Judaism with the current philosophic systems. In the course of this process Jewish philosophers evolved individual Jewish theologies as the result of a synthesis of Judaism and the teachings of such philosophers as Plato, Aristotle and their successors. A résumé of the entire subject is given in

PHILOSOPHY, JEWISH 8:500-15

The following are the principal philosophers and philosophical schools with which Judaism came into contact:

Plato 8:551   Alfarabi, Abu Nasr
Aristotle 1:473-74   Mohammed 1:177-78
Neo-Platonism   Avicenna 1:648
   8:150-51   Ghazzali 4:596
              Averroes 1:643

The most important Jewish philosophers or schools of philosophy were

Philosophy, Alexandrian 8:499-500
Philo 8:495-96
Saadia ben Joseph 9:289-91
David ibn Merwan al-Mukammas 3:485
Al-Basir, Joseph ben Abraham 1:158-59
Jeshuah ben Judah 6:81
Israeli, Isaac ben Solomon 5:619-20
Judah Halevi 6:225-29
Ibn Gabirol, Solomon 5:526-27
Bahya ibn Pakuda 2:34-35
Abraham bar Hiyya 1:40-41
Joseph ben Jacob ibn Zaddik 6:191
Ibn Ezra, Abraham 5:523-25
Ibn Daud, Abraham 5:523
Abravanel, Isaac 1:53-54
Maimonides 7:287-92
Bibago, Abraham 2:279
Gersonides 4:592-93
Crescas, Hasdai ben Abraham 3:408-9
Albo, Joseph 1:161-62

The following Christian philosophers or schools of philosophy were influenced by Jewish philosophy:

Albertus Magnus 1:160
Aquinas, Thomas 1:438
Scholasticism 9:417

Of special interest is the relationship between Jews and the noted modern philosophers

Kant, Immanuel 6:308-9
Hegel, Georg Wilhelm Friedrich 5:290-91

The following articles or sections of articles are devoted to philosophical problems or expositions:

Accident (philosophic   God, Knowledge of
  concept) 1:70   5:4-5
Angels § III. 1:312   Metaphysics 7:507
Attributes of God,   Revelation 9:147-48
  1:609-10   Theodicy 10:241-42
Creation §4. 3:396-98   Truth 10:317-18
Emanation 4:93-94   Wisdom 10:536-38
Free Will § 5. 4:431

In addition, a large number of the articles listed in the outline on THEOLOGY deal with the same subjects as are treated in Jewish philosophy.

OUTLINE 41:

THE RELIGIOUS CALENDAR

Before proceeding to a study of the customs and ceremonies of Judaism, it is well for the student to have a knowledge of the religious calendar of the Jews, which differs in a number of respects from the current civil calendar. Based on a lunar year corrected to the solar year, and divided into various months, the Jewish calendar fixes the dates of the festivals and other annual occasions. In addition, there are various cycles and groupings of years which have been observed in the course of the history of Judaism.

The general article on the subject is

TIME, MEASURING OF 10:251-53

Details are furnished in the articles

Day 3:493	Sabbatical Year
Week 10:482-83	9:300-1
Months 7:633-34	Jubilee 6:214-15
Ereb 4:151	Chronology 3:193-94
Calendar 2:630-41	Eras 4:149-50
Postponement 8:610	

Of special interest in this connection is the article

Calendar Reform 2:641-42

OUTLINE 42:
CUSTOMS AND CEREMONIES

Judaism is especially rich in customs and ceremonies that lend life and color to every sacred day of the year and to numerous milestones in life. Many of them go back to the earliest stages of Jewish history; others have been developed in the course of the centuries, and some are even very recent. Individual Jews and Jewish groups vary as to the extent to which they observe these forms and customs; but for all of them Jewish ceremonies play a very definite part on the chief occasions of their lives.

An outline of the subject is given in

CEREMONIAL OBJECTS AND INSTITUTIONS 3:103-5

The various customs and ceremonies may be divided conveniently as follows:

A. The Life Span

1. **Birth and Infancy**
   Birth 2:379-80
   Circumcision 3:211-16
   Holle Kreish 5:443
   Redemption of the First-Born 9:98-100

2. **Youth**
   Bar Mitzvah 2:73-75   Confirmation 3:329-30

3. **Adult Life**
   Wedding and Wedding Customs 10:480-82

Mizrah 7:601	Lights 7:60
Mezuzah 7:526-27	Mikveh 7:557
Grace at Meals	Ablutions 1:24-26
5:75-77	Purification 9:35-36
Dedication 3:514-15	Penance 8:425
Laying on of Hands	
6:565-66	

Abstinence and Abstention 1:57-59

4. **Death and Burial**
   Dead, Respect for the 3:501-2
   Burial and Burial Customs 2:594-602

Embalming 4:96	Eulogy 4:193
Funeral 4:477-80	Cremation 3:404-6

   Cemetery 3:75-79 (illus. 1:627; 2:479; 3:235; 4:543; 7:420; 9:193, 282, 367; 10:421, 619)
   Catacombs, Jewish 3:64-66
   Mausoleum 7:415-16
   Tombstones 10:265-67 (illus. 2:566; 3:106; 4:4, 38, 545, 554; 5:487, 639, 640; 6:314; 4:543; 7:420; 9:193, 282, 367; 10:421, 619) 487)
   Epitaphs 4:137-40 (illus. 3:369)

5. **Mourning and Respect for the Dead**
   Mourning and Mourning Customs 8:28-31

Kaddish 6:273-75	Yahrzeit 10:583

   Yahrzeit Light 10:583
   Graves, Visiting of 5:89

B. The Religious Year

6. **The Year as a Whole**
   Tallith 10:159-60
   Phylacteries 8:522-23
   Fringes 4:460-61

7. **Sabbath 9:295-99**

Sabbath Soul 9:300	Oneg Shabbat 8:300
Shalom Alechem	Melavveh Malkah
9:493	7:449
Sabbaths, Special	Habdalah 5:140-43
9:300	Spiceboxes 10:1
Shalashudos 9:493	

Holidays 5:410-16
Holidays, Second Day of 5:416
Pilgrimage Festivals 8:531
Processions 8:650-51

8. **Passover 8:408-10**

Paschal Lamb 8:406	Haggadah, Passover
Leaven, Removal of	§1. 5:156-57
6:580	Had Gadya 5:145-46
Leaven 6:580	Haroseth 5:217
Matzoth 7:413-14	Afikomen 1:106
Seder 9:453-56	Omer 8:299

9. **Shabuoth 9:490-91**

10. **Rosh Hashanah 9:227**

Shofar 9:514-15	Penitential Days
Tashlich 10:177	8:426

11. **Yom Kippur 10:604-5**
    Kappores 6:313

12. **Sukkoth 10:95-97**

Sukkah 10:94-95	Hoshana Rabbah
Lulab 7:234	5:465-66
Ethrog 4:186	

13. **Shemini Atzereth 9:502-3**
    Simhath Torah 9:542

14. **Hanukah 5:209-11**
    Menorah 7:487-90

15. Purim 9:36-42
   Megillah 7:438-40

16. **Minor Festive Occasions**
   New Moon 8:171
   Ab, Fifteenth of 1:9-10
   New Year for Trees 8:175
   Lag Beomer 6:508-9

17. **Fasting and Fast Days 4:249-52**
   Ab, Ninth of 1:10-12
   Tebeth, Tenth of 10:186
   Yom Kippur Katan 10:605

An expression of the spirit underlying the ceremonial observances of Judaism is found in the article

CEREMONIAL LAW 3:94-103

A discussion of the interrelationship of the ceremonies of Judaism and other religions is contained in
   Rites and Ceremonies, Borrowed 9:167-68

OUTLINE 43: LITURGY

The Talmud describes prayer as "the divine service of the heart." As the result of this feeling there developed, in the time of the Second Temple and after, an ordered series of prayers for use in private and public devotion which became the Jewish liturgy. Private prayers were the first to develop, and many of these were later incorporated into the public services. Every Jewish service has certain basic prayers which are an invariable part of the service, and there are such services for various divisions of ordinary days and sacred occasions. The daily working-day service contains the basic prayers and but few additions; the Sabbath, festal and holy day services are rich in special prayers for each occasion. The Jewish liturgy, though unified in structure, is not uniform in practice; in course of time there have arisen many rituals, varying according to the age, the country and the religious viewpoint of the worshipper.

The urge for the personal approach to God is described in

PRAYER 8:617-19

with its underlying ideas of
   Adoration 1:100-1   Devotion 3:557
The spirit of the liturgy is described in

DIVINE SERVICE 3:575-77

A general description of the liturgy is given in

LITURGY 7:139-43

The earliest parts of the liturgy were the

A. Private Prayers

Benedictions 2:167-70
   Sheheheyanu 9:500
Kiddush 6:379-80 (also used in public devotions)
Night Prayer 8:221
Mi Addir 7:527
Marriage Benedictions 7:376-77
Grace at Meals   Haggadah, Passover
   5:75-77   5:156-57
Prayers, Special §3.   Dayyenu 3:494
   8:621   Addir Hu 1:81
Funeral 4:477-80   Ki lo Naeh 6:378
                        Had Gadya 5:145-46

B. Public Services

1. The Basic Prayers

Shema 9:501-2
Eighteen Benedictions 4:22-27
Responses in Divine Service 9:140
   Amen 1:223-24
Psalms, Liturgical 9:18-19
Piyut 8:548-49
   Paytan 8:417-18
   Pizmon 8:549
Kaddish 6:273-75

2. The Principal Services of the Day (arranged in the order of their origin)

Evening Service 4:198
Morning Service 7:651
Afternoon Service 1:110-11
Additional Service 1:82-83
Memorial Service 7:462
   El Male Rahamin 4:42
   Yizkor 10:603-4

3. The Daily Service

Mah Tobu 7:281	Mi Chamocha 7:527-28
Baruch Sheamar 2:98	Hashkibenu 5:236
Yigdal 10:603	Keroboth 6:364-65
Vehu Rahum 10:398	Prayers, Special
Tahanun 10:157	§§ 1 and 2. 8:621
Ahabah Rabbah 1:135	Kedushah 6:353-54
Maaribim 7:258	Mashib Haruah 7:396
Yotzeroth 10:607	Ofannim 8:285
Emeth Veyatzib 4:99	Bammeh Madlikin
(known also as	2:61-62
Geullah Prayer	Alenu 1:166-67
4:595)	

4. Special Features of the Sabbath (and sometimes Festival) Service

Kabbalath Shabbath	Nishmath Kol Hai
6:272-73	8:223
Lechah Dodi 6:584-85	Shochen Ad 9:513
Zemiroth 10:638	Zulath 10:677

Torah, Reading of 10:273-76 (for details of this part of the service, see the outline on SYNAGOGUE)

Baruch Shepetarani
2:98
Yekum Purkan 10:588
Healing, Prayers for
5:263
Prayer for the

Government 8:619
Ashre 1:545-46
En Kelohenu 4:102
Adon Olam 1:98-99
Shir Hayihud 9:511
Anim Zemiroth 1:319

5. Special Features of the Festival Services

Priestly Blessing
8:634-35
Hallel 5:183-84

Akdamuth 1:143
Azharoth 1:652-53

6. Special Features of Rosh Hashanah and Yom Kippur Services

Selihoth 9:470
Abinu Malkenu 1:23
Hai Vekayam 5:167
Veyeethayu 10:411
Unethanneh Tokef
10:342-43
Vechol Maaminim
10:398
Malchuyoth 7:304
Zichronoth 10:642
Akedah 1:143-44

Shofaroth 9:515
Kol Nidre 6:440-41
Yaaleh 10:582
Omnam Ken 8:299
Confession § 2.
3:328-29
Ashamnu 1:537
Abodah 1:29-30
Neilah 8:148-49
El Nora Alilah 4:42

7. Special Features for Services on Other Occasions

Al Hanissim 1:152
Maoz Tzur 7:343
Lamentations, Litur-
gical 6:515-16

Eli Zion 4:66-67
El Melech Yosheb
4:42

8. Biblical Characters Especially Mentioned in the Liturgy

Abraham § 3. 1:37-38   Elijah § 3. 4:75-76
The development of the liturgy resulted in the compiling and publication of

PRAYER-BOOKS 8:619-21

The history of this development is further traced in the following articles:

Amram ben Sheshna
1:282-83
Mahzor Vitry 7:285

Abudraham, David
1:60
Rituals 9:170-71
Likkute Zebi 7:61

The literature written as an aid to private worship is treated under

Literature, Devotional 7:85-86

See also the outline on CUSTOMS AND CEREMONIES.

OUTLINE 44: ETHICS AND MORALITY

One of the great contributions of Judaism to religion and civilization is its emphasis on right conduct as the essence of true religion. It was the first religion to make ethics and morality an integral part of its teaching and to bind them closely to its doctrinal beliefs. The ethical motive appears in the earliest legislation and it was given a powerful impetus by the prophetic movement. It continued through the work of the sages and rabbis, who built up an ethical system based on the highest moral principles.

The general articles on the subject are

ETHICS 4:174-81

MORALITY 7:640-41

The individual articles in the field can be grouped around the following heads:

1. Ethical Ideals

Truth 10:317-18
Justice 6:268-70
Righteousness 9:165
Holiness 5:416-18

Altruism 1:214-15
Honor 5:451
Temperance 10:193

2. The Emotions

Love 7:210-11
Hate 5:248
Humility 5:481-82
Jealousy 6:49

Joy 6:213-14
Anger 1:314-16
Gratitude 5:84
Pity 8:547-48

3. Relations to Others

Patience 8:413
Friendship 4:460
Admonition 1:98
Amity 1:275-76
Hospitality 5:466-67
Charity 3:113-14

Strangers 10:71
Heathens 5:269
Gentiles 4:533-34
Enemy 4:108-9
Forgiveness 4:357
Apology 1:427

4. Duties to the Community

Obedience 8:263-64
Responsibility, Collective 9:140-41
Kiddush Hashem and Hillul Hashem 6:380-81

5. Ethical Issues in Life

Riches 9:157-58
Poverty 8:611
War 10:449-52
Conscription 3:335-36

Peace 8:418-21
Birth Control 2:380-81
Labor 6:497-504

6. Ethical Literature

The general article on the subject is
Literature, Ethical 7:86-87

The following articles deal with ethical writers and writings, arranged in chronological order:

Wisdom Literature 10:538
Aboth 1:32-33
Aboth de Rabbi Nathan 1:34
Ibn Gabirol, Solomon 5:526-27
Bahya ibn Pakuda 2:34-35
Judah ben Samuel of Regensburg 6:224
Gerondi, Jonah 4:586-87
Berechiah Hanakdan 2:194-95
Aboab, Isaac, the Elder 1:28-29
Alami, Solomon 1:154
Al-nakawa, Israel 1:196
Bahya ben Asher 2:34

6. Ethical Literature—*Continued*

Eleazar ben Judah 4:61-62
Wills, Ethical 10:523-24
Kahan, Israel Meir 6:282-83
Musar Movement 8:43-44
Orehoth Zaddikim 8:320

OUTLINE 45: JEWISH MYSTICISM

Mysticism was always present in Jewish thought, but it was not until after the 13th century that it became an important factor in Judaism, leaving its impress upon the prayers and ceremonies. A unique factor in Jewish mysticism is the self-abnegation of its votaries, who seldom dwell on their mystic experiences. The literature is frequently anonymous or ascribed to a great teacher of ancient times, so that it is frequently difficult to date individual works of Jewish mystical literature.

The comprehensive article on the subject is

MYSTICISM 8:73-76

The authoritative system which developed is known as

CABALA 2:614-20

An interesting by-product of the latter was
  Cabala, Christian 2:620-21
Mystic experience is described in the articles
  Ascension 1:531   Ecstasy 3:623
Articles dealing with mystical doctrines are
  Sefiroth 9:459
  Man, Primordial 7:311
  Emanation 4:93-94
  Ages of the World 1:118-19
  Alphabet in Mysticism 1:205-6
  Numbers in Mysticism 8:249-51

The following articles, which follow chronological order as nearly as can be ascertained, give a history of Jewish mysticism in terms of speculation, literature and individual mystics:

Hermes, Books of 5:325
Merkabah 7:493-94
Shiur Komah 9:511
Yetzirah, Book of 10:596-97
Akiba, Alphabet of 1:144
Aaron ben Samuel Hanasi 1:5
Ben Sirach, Alphabet of 2:160
Isaac the Blind 5:592
Azriel ben Menahem 1:654
Bahir 2:33
Abulafia, Abraham 1:60-62
Zohar 10:670-71
Hakanah Book 5:172
Alkabetz, Solomon 1:185
Luria, Isaac 7:237-39
Vital, Hayim 10:429
Cordovero, Moses 3:367-68
Horovitz, Isaiah Halevi 5:457
Raziel, Book of 9:88

Many of the ideas found in Cabala were taken over into
  Hasidism 5:237-41

OUTLINE 46: ANGELS AND DEMONS

Ideas about angels and demons range all the way from religion to folklore. In the case of angels, the ideas are generally religious, for they are part of the concept of God as envisioned by the prophets and taught by the philosophers, and it is only with the spread of mysticism that folklore elements appear. Demons, on the other hand, are nearly always an expression of folklore, save in some special instance, such as that of Satan, the accuser, who appears in the pages of the Bible not as a spirit of evil but as one of the servants of God.

The articles in this field can be grouped as follows:

ANGELS 1:304-14

Cherub 3:132-33
Seraphim 9:481
Ofannim 8:285
Recording Angel 9:95
Angel of Death 1:302-3
Azrael 1:654
Accuser 1:70-71
Sanegor 9:361
Metatron 7:507
Gabriel 4:488
Michael 7:529
Raphael 9:72
Uriel 10:381
Sandalphon 9:359
Samael 9:334
Raziel 9:88

DEMONS 3:529-34

Satan 9:379-80
Beelzebub 2:132
Azazel 1:651-52
Ashmodai 1:545
Lilith 7:63

OUTLINE 47: SECTS AND DIVISIONS IN JUDAISM

In the course of Jewish history there have been numerous instances of the rise of individual movements which have tended to divide Jewry and in some cases have resulted in creating separate sects. Such movements generally occurred in periods of spiritual stagnation or at times when a new environment called for readjustments in Jewish life and ideas. Even in cases where the new movement itself eventually withered, its very existence stimulated and revitalized Jewish thought.

The general articles dealing with the subject are

SECTS 9:453
HERESY 5:320-21
CONTROVERSIES 3:339-41

The only sect of importance in Bible times was that of the
  Rechabites 9:93-94

In the period of the Second Temple, there arose the sect of

Samaritans 9:335-39

The following articles deal with Samaritan leaders or literature:

Dositheus 3:591
Joshua, Samaritan Book of 6:206-7
Secrets of Moses 9:453

The chief division in the 3rd and first half of the 2nd century B.C.E. was between

Hellenism 5:306-7   Hasideans 5:237

After the triumph of the Maccabees and the restoration of independence (165 B.C.E.) the three important sects were

Sadducees 9:308-9

Boethusians 2:438   Herodians 5:327

Pharisees 8:473-76

(for a list of the Pharisaic leaders, see the outline in TALMUD, under the subhead: The Chain of Tradition)

Essenes 4:167-68

Hemerobaptists 5:313-14

The chief division in the last century C.E. was between

Beth Hillel and Beth Shammai 2:251-52

A new sect seeking independence arose as the

Zealots 10:630-31

Sicarii 9:525

During the period of the Mishnah (until 200 C.E.) groups which did not follow the standard teachings of Judaism were known as

Minim 7:567-68   Am Haaretz 1:216-18
Epicurus 4:136-37

The Jewish sects of the Middle Ages were those of

Yudghan 10:617

Karaites 6:314-19

The latter called their opponents and the latter's teaching

Rabbinites 9:56   Rabbinism 9:56

The most important Karaite leaders, arranged in chronological order, were

Anan ben David 1:293
Benjamin ben Moses Nahavendi 2:179
Daniel ben Moses al-Kumisi 3:467
Solomon ben Jeroham 9:637-38
Kirkisani, Jacob 6:397-98
David ben Abraham Alfasi 3:483
Yefet ben Ali Halevi 10:587
Albasir, Joseph 1:158-59
Jeshuah ben Judah 6:81
Dari, Moses 3:470-71
Hadasi, Judah 5:147
Tobiah ben Moses 10:258
Ali ibn Suleiman 1:183-84
Aaron ben Joseph 1:4
Aaron ben Elijah of Nicomedia 1:2-4
Bashyazi, Elijah ben Moses 2:104
Afendopolo, Caleb 1:105
Bashyazi, Moses ben Elijah 2:104

Troki, Isaac 10:311
Kokisow, Mordecai 6:440
Luzki, Simhah Isaac ben Moses 7:244
Firkovitch, Abraham 4:312-13

An interesting Karaite sect was that of

Abele Zion 1:18-20

In modern times the first movement of importance was

Hasidism 5:237-41

The later development of the Hasidic movement is treated under

Zaddik and Zaddikism 10:623-24

The chief Hasidic leaders, arranged in chronological order, were

Baal Shem, The 2:3-5
Baer of Meseritz 2:28
Jacob Joseph Hakohen of Polonnoye 6:12-13
Elimelech of Lizianka 4:77
Aaron of Karlin 1:5-6
Abraham Hamalach 1:43
Menahem Mendel of Vitebsk 7:466
Menahem Nahum of Tchernobyl 7:466-67
Levi Isaac of Berdichev 6:622
Israel of Kozience 5:617
Shneur Zalman ben Baruch of Liady 9:512
Baruch of Miedzybozh 2:97-98
Nahman ben Simhah of Bratzlav 8:86
Baer of Liubavich 2:27
Moses Löb of Sassow 8:11
Spira 10:9
Teitelbaum, Moses 10:188
Ruzhiner, Israel 9:288-89
Menahem Mendel of Kock 7:465-66
Menahem Mendel of Liubavich 7:466
Gerer Rebbe 4:540
Leiner 6:600-1
David ben Mordecai 3:484
Baer of Leovo 2:27
Yablonaer Rebbe 10:582-83

The movements of the 19th and 20th centuries were

Reform Movement 9:101-3

Haskalah 5:242-45

Musar Movement 8:43-44

Zionism (treated in a special outline) 10:645-67

Jewish Science 6:142

The main movements in the United States: Reform, Conservatism, Orthodoxy and Reconstructionism, are treated in detail in

JUDAISM IN AMERICA 6:237-46

Rabbinical organizations of the various groups are

Central Conference of American Rabbis 3:88-92
Rabbinical Assembly of America 9:53-55
Rabbinical Council of America 9:55
Union of Orthodox Rabbis of the United States and Canada 10:346-47

PART IV: JEWISH LIFE

OUTLINE 48: FAMILY AND SOCIAL LIFE

Every observer of the Jews has noted the strength of their family and social ties and the richness of their family and social life. These phenomena have resulted partly from the strong tradition of family and social solidarity which has been handed down among the Jews since ancient times and partly from outside pressure which has kept the Jews a compact unit. The purpose of this outline is to treat the principles underlying family and social relationships and to describe their outstanding features.

A general article on the family is

FAMILY AND FAMILY LIFE 4:242-44

The home and some of its features are described in

House 5:473-74	Mizrah 7:601
Lamp 6:516-18	Mezuzah 7:526-27
Weights and Measures 10:484	

The relations of the sexes in general are treated in
Sex Laws and Customs 9:487-89
Woman 10:564-69

The various types of marriage are described in

Monogamy 7:623	Concubine 3:324-25
Polygamy 8:584-85	

The preliminaries leading up to marriage are dealt with in

Eugenics 4:191-92	Betrothal 2:254-55
Shadhan 9:491	Dowry 3:592-93

The laws and customs relating to marriage are given in

Marriage 7:369-76	Halitzah 5:180-83
Levirate Marriage 6:638	Kethubah 6:367-72

The wedding ceremony itself is described in
Wedding and Wedding Customs 10:480-82
Huppah 5:504-5
Veiling of the Bride 10:399

A custom of having the married couple live for some time with their parents is described in
Kest 6:366

The ideal of marriage is treated in
Chastity 3:120-22

The violation of this ideal, in
Adultery §2. 1:103   Mamzer 7:309

Abstention from marriage is discussed in
Celibacy 3:72-73

The relations of parents and children are treated in such articles as
Childlessness 3:153
Adoption 1:100
Pregnancy 8:629-30

Parents and Children 8:398
Parental Blessing 8:397
Parental Authority 8:397
Wills, Ethical 10:523-24

Most of the ceremonies observed in the home are of a religious nature, and are treated in the outline on CUSTOMS AND CEREMONIES.

The chief personal observance was
Birthday 2:382

The following articles deal with social relations:

Brother 2:557-58	Drunkenness 3:603
Manners 7:329-30	Sick, Visiting of
Decorum 3:513-14	9:527
Blessing 2:391-93	Slavery 9:566
Kiss and Kissing 6:405-6	Strangers 10:71
Greeting and Wish	Letters and Letter
Formulas 5:99-100	Writers 6:615-17
	Ghetto 4:597-603

OUTLINE 49: COSTUME

There never has been any universally followed or generally distinct Jewish costume. However, in various countries and in various periods Jews have either been forced to wear certain garments to distinguish them from non-Jews or have shown a preference for certain marked styles of dress. It frequently happened that Jews who migrated from one country to another retained the old national dress of their former home for so long a period that it came to be regarded as a distinctly Jewish garb. With emancipation and entrance into all fields of endeavor Jews always eventually came to dress in the same fashion as their neighbors.

The general article dealing with the subject is

COSTUMES 3:375-81

Related articles on the general subject of dress and ornament are

Clothing, Regulations Concerning 3:224-25	
Fringes 4:460-61	Wig 10:517-18
Head, Covering of 5:262-63	Cosmetics 3:371-72
Beard 2:123-24	Ornamentation 8:326-27
Side-Locks 9:527-28	Ring 9:165-66
Shaving 9:497	Seal 9:449

OUTLINE 50: DIET AND HYGIENE

The superior longevity of the Jews as compared to their neighbors has been attributed to their care for diet and hygiene. This outline comprises the articles which contain information in this field.

The following foods and beverages receive separate articles

Milk 7:561   Egg 4:4-5
Honey 5:450   Bread 2:516
Wine 10:528-29

The baking of bread is treated in
Baking 2:37-38   Hallah 5:183
Other foods are enumerated in
Cooking 3:347-52

The dietary laws observed by Orthodox Jews are described in

Dietary Laws 3:564
Mixtures, Prohibited 7:598-99
The enforcement of their observance is given also in

Kashruth 6:327-31
Slaughtering, Ritual 9:562-65
Mashgiah 7:396   Hechsher 5:288
The hygiene of the Jews is treated from the point of view of religious law in

Purity, Ritual 9:42-43
from the point of view of medicine in
Hygiene of the Jews 5:509-14
and from the point of view of sociology in
Social Hygiene of the Jews 9:578-79
The following articles deal with diseases:
Leprosy 6:610-11   Malaria 7:302-3
Plague 8:549-50
Hygienic bathing is treated under
Bathing 2:108   Mikveh 7:557
Other articles in the field of hygiene are
Birth 2:379-80   Menstruation 7:490-91
Organizations for the promotion of hygiene among Jews are
OSE 8:332-33
Red Magen David 9:96

OUTLNE 51: JEWISH MUSIC

Jewish music falls into two main categories: religious and folk music. Both forms go back to the time when the Jews were still living in Palestine, yet in the course of years Jewish folk and synagogue music alike absorbed many elements from their surroundings. The music of Jews in different countries varies greatly, though a number of typical and widespread tunes have been described and recorded by modern Jewish musicologists.

The music of the Jews in ancient times is treated under

Music in the Bible 8:46-48
The musical reading of the Torah is described in
Cantillation 3:14-15
That for the prayers is discussed in
Niggun 8:221
That for study is treated in
Gemara Niggun 4:525
Secular Jewish music is treated in

FOLK SONGS 4:350-55

Hatikvah 5:249
Music in the Synagogue is treated under

MUSIC, SYNAGOGAL 8:48-55

Cantor 3:17-18   Choir 3:162-63
Congregational Singing 3:331-32
Organ 8:321-22
Specimens of Jewish music are given also in the following articles:

Addir Hu 1:81   Keroboth 6:365
Adon Olam 1:99   Kiddush 6:379
Alenu 1:167   Kol Nidre 6:440-41
Ashamnu 1:537   Lechah Dodi 6:584-85
Hoshana Rabbah   Maoz Tzur 7:343
  5:465-66   Purim 9:40
Kaddish 6:275   Sabbath 9:299
Kedushah 6:354

The following are the most important Jewish cantors:

Lowy, Israel 7:220-21 (G, F)
Weintraub, Shlomo 10:491-92 (Ru, A)
Straschunsky, Joel Dovid 10:74 (Ru, Po)
Sulzer, Salomon 10:101-2 (A)
Naumbourg, Samuel 8:132-33 (F)
Abrass, Joshua 1:52-53 (Ru, A)
Deutsch, Moritz 3:555 (A, G)
Lewandowski, Louis 7:20-21 (G)
Wasserzug, Chayim 10:474 (Po, E)
Schorr, Boruch 9:423 (A)
Baer, Abraham 2:28-29 (G, Sw)
Spivak, Nisen 10:15 (Ru)
Kaiser, Alois 6:292 (US)
Singer, Josef 9:556 (G, A)
Gerowitsch, Eliezer 4:587 (Ru)
Rozowski, Boruch Leib 9:267-68 (Ru, Latvia)
Razumni, Solomon 9:89 (Ru)
Birnbaum, Eduard 2:369 (G)
Stark, Edward 10:21 (US)
Minkowsky, Pinchos 7:570-71 (Ru, US)
Friedmann, Aaron 4:457 (G)
Kirschner, Emanuel 6:398-99 (G)
Sparger, William 9:695 (US)
Maragowsky, Jacob Samuel 7:345-46 (Ru, US)
Rosenblatt, Josef 9:210 (Hu, US)
Goldfarb, Israel 5:21 (US)
Roitman, David 9:183 (Ru, US)
Jassinowsky, Pinchos 6:42-43 (Ru, US)
Weisser, Samuel 10:494 (Ru, US)
Kwartin, Savel 6:494 (Ru, A, Hu, US)

Articles on students of Jewish music are
Binder, Abraham Wolf 2:354 (US)
Idelsohn, Abraham Zevi 5:534-35
(G, S Af, US)
Nadel, Arno 8:81 (G)
Saminsky, Lazare 9:339-40 (Ru, US)
Singer, Jacob 9:556 (US)

OUTLINE 52:

STRIKING JEWISH PHRASES

In the course of their centuries of history Jews have developed a number of striking phrases which were once used as part of their daily speech and which in many cases have survived even when Jews have adopted the same language as their neighbors. Other noteworthy expressions have been adopted from the language of the Bible or the Talmud. These and similar expressions are grouped in this outline.

The following articles contain lists of various types of phrases in frequent use:
Phrases, Biblical 8:519-20
Phrases, Talmudic 8:521
Phrases, Popular 8:520-21
Greeting and Wish Formulas 5:99-100

The following phrases are given special articles:
Aberah 1:21
Aliyah 1:184-85
Amen 1:223-24
Baal § 2. 2:2-3
Baal Habayith 2:3
Baal Shem 2:3
Baal Teshubah 2:5
Bar 2:69
Belaaz 2:144
Belial 2:151
Ben 2:156
Bene Israel 2:164-65
(see also Children of Israel 3:154)
Benshen 2:186
Bosheth 2:479
Daughter of Zion 3:475
Davnen 3:492
Din 3:566
Ereb 4:151
Eretz Israel 4:152
Galuth 4:502
Haggadah 5:155-56
Halachah 5:172-75
Javan 6:47
Kosher 6:459
Maggid 7:272-73
Mammon 7:308
Mazal 7:427
Mitzvah 7:591-93
Nittel 8:224-25
Pilpul 8:532
Schnorrer 9:415
Shlemiel and Shlimazzel 9:511
Siyum 9:560-61
Tikkun 10:250-51
Zaddik 10:623

OUTLINE 53: AMUSEMENTS

This outline deals with the favorite sports and relaxations favored by the Jews for their entertainment from the earliest to modern times. The more active amusements were
Athletics § 1. 1:581-84
Dance 3:455-63

The sedentary amusements are described in
Games 4:509   Trendel 10:300
Gambling 4:508
Chess 3:133-34 (see also the separate outline JEWS IN CHESS)
Meals, Festal 7:428

The intellectual amusements are treated in
Riddle 9:160-61
Words, Play on 10:572-73
Gematria 4:525-26
Wit and Humor, Jewish 10:545-48

The purveyors of jests, especially at weddings, were known as
Badhan 2:25-26   Marshalik 7:379

OUTLINE 54: JEWISH EDUCATION

Jewish education has been a most important factor in preserving Judaism in the midst of a different and often hostile environment. Jewish doctrines and teachings were handed down from generation to generation by a system of education that began in ancient times and has continued to the present and which was impressed upon child and adult alike. The maintenance of teachers and pupils was a community obligation and a carefully graded system of schools, varied according to the needs of the time, was created to provide for the instruction and guidance of every individual.

The spirit underlying Jewish education is treated in the article

STUDY 10:90-91

The comprehensive article on the subject is

EDUCATION 3:629-40

Articles dealing with various types of schools are
Schools 9:420-22
Beth Hamidrash 2:250-51
Be Rab 2:122
Academies 1:63-67
Kallah Months 6:297-98
Talmud Torah 10:167
Yeshiva 10:592-95
Klaus 6:410-11
Teachers' Training Schools 10:185-86
Rabbinical Seminaries 9:55-56
Types of teachers are discussed in
Teachers 10:184-85
Soferim 9:587
Gaon and Gaonic Period 4:513-14
Types of students are described in the articles
Students, Types of 10:88-90
Bahur 2:33-34
An important aid to study was
Mnemonics 7:601-2

Textbooks are mentioned frequently in the articles in this outline, and in addition there is an article on

Catechisms, Jewish 3:66-67

The articles on various modern Jewish schools and school systems may be grouped as follows:

1. Rabbinical Seminaries

Aria College 1:472
Collegio Rabbinico Italiano 3:264
Emanu-El Theological Seminary 4:94
Hebrew Theological College of Chicago 5:282
Hebrew Union College 5:282-83
Hochschule für die Wissenschaft des Judentums 5:405
Jewish Institute of Religion 6:132-33
Jewish Theological Seminary of America 6:143-47
Jews' College 6:148-49
Jüdisch-Theologisches Seminar 6:264
Maimonides College 7:296
Nederlandsch Israelietisch Seminarium 8:141
Országos Rabbiképző Intézet 8:329
Portugeesch-Israelietisch Seminarium Ets Haim 8:607-8
Rabbinerseminar für das orthodoxe Judentum 9:53
Séminaire Israélite 9:473

2. Institutions for Jewish Studies

Akademie für die Wissenschaft des Judentums 1:142-43 (G)
College of Jewish Studies 3:264 (US)
Dropsie College 3:600-2 (US)
Gratz College 5:87-88 (US)
Judith Lady Montefiore College 6:265 (E)

A combination of general studies with Jewish studies and a rabbinical seminary is found in

Yeshiva College 10:595-96 (US)

Institutions giving a secular, vocational and sometimes a Jewish education are

Ahlem 1:140-41 (G)
Bezalel School 2:274-75 (P)
Graduate School for Jewish Social Work, The 5:78-80 (US)
Hebrew University of Jerusalem 5:284-87 (P)
National Farm School, The 8:119-20 (US)
Philanthropin 8:484 (G)

A noteworthy system of girls' schools is

Beth Jakob Schools 2:252 (Po, A, Lithuania, Latvia, P)

The following are important Jewish educators of modern times, arranged in chronological order

Homberg, Herz 5:448 (A)
Stern, Basilius 10:53 (Ru)
Rée, Anton 9:100 (G)
Angel, Moses 1:303-4 (E)
Schnabel, Louis 9:412 (A, F, US)
Baar, Herman 2:5-6 (G, E, Be, US)
Baerwald, Hermann 2:29-30 (G, A)

Steinberg, Joshua 10:43 (Lithuania)
Sulzberger, David 10:99 (US)
Blaustein, David 2:390 (US)
Berkowitz, Henry 2:204-5 (US)
Friedland, Abraham Hyman 4:451 (US)
Elbogen, Ismar (d. 1943) 4:44-45 (G, US)
Benderly, Samson 2:164 (US)
Adler, Herbert M. (d. 1940) 1:93 (E)
Magnes, Judah Leon 7:276-77 (US, P)
Kaplan, Mordecai M. 6:311 (US)
Hurwitz, Henry 5:506 (US)
Dushkin, Alexander M. 3:613-14 (US, P)
Safir, Shelley Ray 9:311 (US)
Chipkin, Israel S. 3:160-61 (US)
Berkson, Isaac B. 2:206 (US)
Soltes, Mordecai 9:644 (US)
Honor, Leo Lazarus 5:451-52 (US)
Scharfstein, Zevi 9:391 (US)
Gamoran, Emanuel 4:510 (US)
Golub, Jacob S. 5:48-49 (US)
Maller, Julius B. 7:305 (US)
Franzblau, Abraham Norman 4:418-19 (US)

The following are organizations devoted to Jewish education:

Jewish Chautauqua Society 6:94-95
Jewish Education, American Association for 6:128-29
Jewish Education Committee 6:129-30
National Council for Jewish Education 8:116
Tarbuth 10:172

The following organizations were founded to create interest in Jewish studies or to encourage Jewish schools:

Institut zur Förderung der Israelitischen Literatur 5:575
Institut Nauk Judaistycznych 5:576
Ivriah 5:644
Jewish Academy of Arts and Sciences 6:90-91
Jewish Information Bureau 6:131
Société des Études Juives 9:586
Society for Jewish Jurisprudence 9:586
Verein für Cultur und Wissenschaft des Judentums 10:405
Yiddish Scientific Institute 10:602-3

OUTLINE 55: SYNAGOGUE

Ever since its first beginnings the synagogue has played an essential part in the Jewish community, in its triple role of house of prayer, house of study, and house of assembly. Most of these functions are treated elsewhere in such outlines as LITURGY, EDUCATION, CUSTOMS AND CEREMONIES, and COMMUNITY AND COMMUNAL ORGANIZATIONS. This outline deals with certain features which distinguish the synagogue.

The general article on the subject is

SYNAGOGUE 10:119-30

Articles dealing with the architecture and furnishing of the synagogue are
Architecture 1:466-67
Weiberschul 10:483
Frescoes and Murals 4:438-41
Ark (in the synagogue) 1:475-77
Parocheth 8:403
Torah, Scroll of 10:276-77
Torah, Ornamentation of 10:269-73
Perpetual Light 8:460
Pulpit 9:35
Menorah 7:487-90
Almemar 1:193

The disputed question of the organ in the synagogue is treated in
Organ 8:321-22

Worship in the synagogue is described in such articles as
Minyan 7:577-78
Divine Service 3:575-77
Congregational Singing 3:331-32
and other articles listed in the outline on LITURGY.

The following articles deal with the reading of the Scriptures in the synagogue:
Sidra 9:528-29
Parashah 8:393-96
    Parashahs, The Four 8:396
Haftarah 5:152-53
Torah, Reading of 10:273-76
Shnoddern 9:513
Hathan Torah 5:248-49
Hathan Bereshith 5:248

The sermon, which began as an exposition of the Scriptures read in the synagogue, is treated in
Sermon 9:481-82   Darshan 3:474
Preaching 8:622-23   Maggid 7:272-73
Homiletics 5:449

Synagogue organizations described in special articles are
Agudath Israel 1:128-31
Jewish Sabbath Alliance of America 6:141-42
National Council of Young Israel 8:119
National Federation of Jewish Men's Clubs of the United Synagogue of America 8:120
National Federation of Temple Brotherhoods 8:120-21
National Federation of Temple Sisterhoods 8:121-22
Society for the Advancement of Judaism 9:586
Union of American Hebrew Congregations 10:344-45
Union Libérale Israélite 10:346
Union of Orthodox Jewish Congregations of America 10:346
Union of Sephardic Congregations 10:347
United Synagogue of America 10:352-53

World Union for Progressive Judaism 10:575-76
Young Israel 10:607

OUTLINE 56: COMMUNITY AND COMMUNAL ORGANIZATION

Jewish community organization started in Palestine at the time when the Jews had their own government; it was retained in the Diaspora, since Judaism was a recognized religion and the Jews were allowed to form their own organizations. This condition prevailed all through the Middle Ages, and was particularly important when the Jews were forcibly segregated into ghettos or constituted a distinct group within a country. In modern times, communal organization has become more voluntary and possesses less power, but nevertheless is a tremendously important factor in Jewish life.

The general article dealing with the subject is

JEWISH COMMUNITY AND COMMUNAL ORGANIZATIONS 6:99-126

The other articles in this field may be grouped as follows:

1. The Jewish Community in Bible Times
Elders 4:46
King and Kingdom 6:384-86
Tithe 10:253-54

2. The Jewish Community in the Talmudic Period
Gerusia 4:593-94   Apostoloi 1:432
Ethnarch 4:185   Exilarch 4:207-9
Tetrarch 10:203   Bostanai 2:480
Sanhedrin 9:361-63   Pater Synagogae 8:412
Maamadoth 7:257-58   Archisynagogue 1:466
Patriarchate   Burial Society
    8:413-14   2:603-4

3. The Jewish Community in the Middle Ages
Kahal 6:279-82
Fattori (del Ghetto) 4:254
Shtadlan 9:520
Bishop of the Jews 2:383-84
Mahamad 7:281

4. The Jewish Community in Modern Times
Consistory 3:336
Crown Rabbi 3:426
Kehillah Movement 6:354-56
Synagogue 10:119-30
Congregation 3:331
Center, The Jewish 3:84-88
Community Councils 3:321-22

5. Community Government
Self-Government 9:466
Takkanoth 10:157-58
Anathema 1:294-96
Excommunication 4:205-6

6. Functionaries, Religious and Communal
4:470-77

Rabbi and Rabbinate 9:48-53
   Ordination 8:318-20
Cantor 3:17-18
Chaplains, Jewish § 2. 3:112

7. Community Records

Archives, Communal   Memorbuch 7:461
  1:467-69   Martyrology 7:387-88
Pinkas 8:535-36

8. Community Titles

Titles 10:254-55   Berabbi 2:190
Haber 5:143   Hacham Bashi 5:145
Abba 1:13-14

9. Community Characters

Batlan 2:112-13   Schnorrer 9:415
Shlemiel and Shlimazzel 9:511

The following articles deal with most important organizations (not including those mentioned in other outlines) in modern Jewish communities:

a. Of International Scope

Alliance Israélite Universalle 1:88-92
Comité des Délégations Juives 3:312-13
Women's Organizations 10:569-70
World Jewish Congress 10:575
Youth Movements 10:612-17

b. In Argentine

Delegación de Asociaciones Israelitas
    Argentinas 3:517

c. In Austria

Allianz, Israelitische, zu Wien 1:192
Union österreichischer Juden 10:347

4. In England

Anglo-Jewish Association 1:317-18
Board of Deputies of British Jews 2:428-30
Jewish Memorial Council 6:134
League of British Jews 6:572
Maccabeans, The 7:260

e. In Germany

Central-Verein deutscher Staatsbürger
    jüdischen Glaubens 3:93
Hilfsverein der Deutschen Juden 5:360-62
Jüdischer Kulturbund 6:263-64
Reichsbund jüdischer Frontsoldaten 9:115-16
Reichsvertretung der deutschen Juden 9:116

f. In Roumania

Uniunea Evreilor Pamanteni 10:353

g. In the United States: General

American Jewish Committee 1:242-47
American Jewish Congress 1:247-53
Board of Delegates of American Israelites
    2:427
Board of Delegates of Civil and Religious
    Rights 2:427-28

Conference on Jewish Relations 3:326-27
General Jewish Council 4:527-28
Jewish War Veterans of the United States
    6:147
Jewish Welfare Board 6:147-48
National Association of Jewish Center
    Workers 8:113-14
National Council of Jewish Women 8:116-18
Synagogue Council of America 10:131-32
Young Men's and Young Women's Hebrew
    Associations 10:608

h. In the United States: By Country of Origin

Galician Jews of America, United 4:499-500
Hungarian Jews of America, Association of
    5:482-83
Hungarian Jews of America, Federation of
    5:483
Lithuanian Jews, Federation of 7:137
Polish Jews in America, Federation of 8:580
Roumanian Jews of America, United 9:265

i. Fraternal Orders

B'nai B'rith 2:422-27
    Anti-Defamation League 1:336
    Hillel Foundations 5:363-67
    National Jewish Monthly 8:123
Brith Abraham, Independent Order of 2:532-34
Brith Sholom 2:534
Free Sons of Israel, The 4:427-28
Jewish National Workers Alliance of America
    6:138
Order Sons of Zion 8:318
Probus National 8:649

For fraternal organizations among American Jewish university students, see
    Fraternities, Jewish 4:423-25

j. Agricultural Associations

Jewish Farmers of America, Federation of
    6:130
Jewish Farmers Association of Palestine
    6:130-31

A number of other organizations of more local importance are listed in the various articles dealing with countries and communities. There are numerous other Jewish organizations which are devoted to the furthering of some specific cause. These are listed in the outline pertaining to that subject, such as those on EDUCATION, SYNAGOGUE, SOCIAL WELFARE, SECTS AND DIVISIONS and the like.

OUTLINE 57: SOCIAL WELFARE

There has always been a strong feeling of social responsibility among the Jews. In ancient times family and group solidarity, as well as the ethical teachings of the prophets and sages, created a system of legislation which provided for the poor, the orphan and the helpless. In the Diaspora and down to the present the need for the aid of less fortunate brethren at home and in foreign lands has stimulated the Jew to philanthropic and social endeavor which has become the model for all types of social work. The ethical and religious basis which underlies the Jewish idea of social welfare, as well as some of the methods used, are described in

CHARITY 3:113-14
PHILANTHROPY 8:484-85

The expression of these ideals in the form found in Jewish law is given in

SOCIAL LEGISLATION 9:579-80

Modern forms of social welfare work are summarized in

SOCIAL SERVICE, JEWISH 9:580-83

The modes of collecting and distributing funds for social welfare are treated in the articles

Kuppah 6:490   Federations 4:264-65
Tamhui 10:168   United Jewish Appeal
Charity-Box 3:114   10:348

Foundations created by philanthropic Jewish individuals are enumerated in

Foundations, American Jewish 4:361-63

The following are types of personal aid and corresponding institutions:

Aged, Care of 1:111-14
Child Care 3:149-51
National Home for Jewish Children 8:122
Sick, Visiting of 9:527
Hekdesh 5:303-4
Hospitals, Jewish 5:467-71
National Jewish Hospital 8:122-23
Jewish Consumptives' Relief Society 6:126
Captives 3:34-35
Jewish Braille Institute of America 6:94
Loans 7:149-50
Hebrew Free Loan Society 5:275-76
Mendicancy 7:481-82
Animals, Protection of 1:330-31

The following are types of work in behalf of the migrants:

Migrations of the Jews § V. 7:554-56
Immigrant Aid 5:544-46
Americanization 1:273-75

Organizations devoted to this purpose are

Hirsch Fund, Baron de 5:371-73
Jewish Colonization Association 6:97-98
Hebrew Sheltering and Immigrant Aid Society 7:555-56
Emigdirect 4:99-100
Hicem 5:356-57
Industrial Removal Office 5:563-64
Jewish Agricultural Society 6:93-94
Jewish Agriculturists' Aid Society 6:94
Jewish Immigrant Aid Society of Canada 6:131

The following organizations were created before or during the first World War and some have functioned since then to aid the Jews of Europe:

Central Relief Committee 3:92-93
Idgeskom 5:535
American Joint Reconstruction Foundation 1:256-58
Joint Distribution Committee, American Jewish 6:170-76
ORT 8:329-31

The following committee is especially concerned with the welfare of the Falashas:

American Pro-Falasha Committee 1:271

Other societies and organizations are devoted to the social welfare of the Jews in the Soviet Union, such as

American Jewish Joint Agricultural Corporation 1:253-56
American Society for Jewish Farm Settlements in Russia 1:271-72
Icor 5:533-34
Komzet 6:445
Ozet 8:340

The following articles deal with aid to refugees from the Nazi terror:

Refugees 9:103-10
National Refugee Service 8:124-26
Refugee Economic Corporation 9:103
Notgemeinschaft 8:246

Institutions which pursue research in social welfare are

Graduate School for Jewish Social Work 5:78-80
Bureau of Jewish Social Research 2:590

The following are organizations of Jewish social workers:

Council of Jewish Federations and Welfare Funds 3:383
National Conference of Jewish Social Welfare 8:115-16
International Conference of Jewish Social Work 5:577-78

OUTLINE 58: JEWISH LAW.

A. SOURCES AND DEVELOPMENT

Judaism as a religion lays particular stress on proper conduct in human relations. The guide to such conduct is the Law or Torah, and successive generations of teachers and interpreters developed this Torah into a system of jurisprudence which covered every human action. This development was largely unrestricted due to the fact that down to modern times Jews were allowed to follow their own laws and utilize their own courts in many instances. From time to time, in order to systemative the vast bulk of

Jewish law, it became necessary to organize it into logically planned codes.

The basis of all Jewish law and the inspiration of its development is

TORAH 10:267-69

The basic commandments are contained in

Commandments, The Ten 3:314-15 (for a critical view of the evolution of the Ten Commandments, *see* Decalogue 3:506-13)

The rabbis singled out certain basic ethical laws, obligatory upon all humanity, as

Noahide Laws 8:227-28

The laws of the Torah were summed up by them as

Precepts, The 613 8:623-29

Those parts of Jewish law which were not contained in the Torah were called

Oral Law 8:317
Sinaitic Laws 9:553-54

The development of Jewish law proceeded in two ways: by interpretation of the basic laws and by the legalization of customs. These processes are treated in the articles

Hermeneutics,	Casuistry 3:63-64
Talmudic 5:323-24	Tradition 10:290-91
Dialectics 3:558	Custom 3:436-37

The two forces that acted as checks and balances on this process were

Authority 1:630-40
Individualism 5:559-63

Difficulties in the interpretation and development of the Law are discussed in

Opinion, Freedom of 8:303-4
Laws, Conflict of 6:564
Law, Abrogation of 6:553

The authoritative law, reached as the result of discussion and weighing of authorities, was known as

Halachah 5:172-75   Din 3:566

A general survey of the historical development of Jewish law is given in

LAW, JEWISH: SOURCES AND DEVELOPMENT OF 6:557-61

The following articles give details of this development:

Midrash 7:538   Mishnah 7:581-82

For a statement of the way in which the systematic arrangement of the Mishnah came about, see

Akiba ben Joseph § 3. 1:148
Talmud 10:160-65
(for details, *see* the outline on TALMUD)

Academies 1:63-67
Gaon and Gaonic Period 4:513-14
Responsa and Decisions 9:137-39
Takkanoth 10:157-58
Codes 3:230-32

The following are the chief Jewish codes and codifiers, in chronological order:

Ahai of Shabba 1:136
Halachoth Pesukoth 5:175
Halachoth Gedoloth 5:175
Hananel ben Hushiel 5:200-1
Hefetz ben Yatzliah 5:290
Alfasi, Isaac ben Jacob 1:178-79
Maimonides 7:292-94
Eleazar ben Judah 4:61-62
Moses ben Jacob of Coucy 8:10
Mordecai ben Hillel 7:642-43
Asher ben Jehiel 1:538-39
Jacob ben Asher 6:9-10
Kol Bo 6:440
Asufoth 1:576-77
Caro, Joseph 3:49-50
Shulhan Aruch 9:521-22
Isserles, Moses 5:622-23
Danzig, Abraham 3:470

OUTLINE 59:   JEWISH LAW.

B.   INDIVIDUAL LAWS AND LEGAL PRINCIPLES

This outline deals primarily with the various topics and conceptions under the general head of law. It is intended to afford an opportunity of contrasting the regulations of Jewish law with those prevalent in modern courts.

The general article on the subject is

LAW, JEWISH: CLASSIFICATION OF 6:554-57

The articles on law may be grouped as follows:

1. General Legal Principles and Enactments

Competency, Legal 3:322	Safety Legislation 9:311
Blindness 2:394	Malfeasance in Office 7:304
Burden of Proof 2:590	Accident (in law) 1:69
Intention 5:577	Error 4:156-57
Abetment 1:21-22	Presumption, Legal 8:633
Accessory to Crime 1:69	
Instigation 5:575	Identification 5:535
Duress 3:612-13	Majority 7:297-98
Danger to Life 3:463-64	Residence, Laws Concerning 9:137
Precedence 8:623	Neighbor 8:148

The sections dealing with *Criminal Law* are

2. Offenses Against Persons

Murder 8:42-43	Abduction 1:18
Parricide 8:403-4	Insult 5:576-77
Suicide 10:93-94	Slander 9:562
Threat 10:248	Calumny 2:647-48
Assault and Battery	Informers 5:564-65
1:553-54	Self-Defense 9:465
Tort 10:281-82	Retaliation, Law of
Rape 9:72	9:142-44

Of interest in this connection is the article
Animals, Protection of 1:320-31

3. Offenses Against Property

Extortion 4:217-18	Robbery 9:174-75
Embezzlement 4:97-98	Burglary 2:592
Theft 10:240	Stolen Goods 10:67-68

The general article dealing with *Civil Law* is

Law, Civil 6:553-54

The following sections come under this head:

4. Domestic and Sexual Relations

Sex Laws and	Katlanith 6:334-35
Customs 9:487-89	Kethubah 6:367-72
Woman 10:564-66	Virgin 10:425
Marriage 7:369-76	Foundling 4:363
Consanguinity	Hermaphrodite
3:334-35	5:322-23
Affinity 1:105-6	Adultery § 1. 1:102-3
Levirate Marriage	Desertion 3:543-44
6:638	Agunah 1:132-33
Halitzah 5:180-83	Divorce 3:577-80
Concubine 3:324-25	Alimony 1:184

5. Inheritance Law

Inheritance 5:565-66	Guardian 5:114
Wills 10:523	Birthright 2:382-83
Widow 10:513	Primogeniture
Orphans 8:328	8:644-45
Mamzer 7:309	Ascendent 1:531

6. Business Law

Contracts and	Surety 10:105-6
Conditions 3:338-39	Assignment 1:555-56
Asmachta 1:552	Good Faith 5:56-57
Partnership 8:405-6	Fraud and Deception
Labor § 7. 6:501-3	4:425-26
Loans 7:149-50	Sham Transaction
Pledge 8:551-52	9:494
Usury 10:385	Overreaching 8:339-40
Debts 3:506	Prosbul 9:1

7. Property Law

Property, Personal	Finding of Property
8:656	4:303-4
Property, Sale and	Possession 8:609
Transfer of 8:656-58	Bailments 2:35
Barter and Sale	Responsibility 9:140
2:93-94	Negligence 8:144-45
Gifts 4:608	Hefker 5:290
Loss 7:203	

8. Real Estate Law

Agriculture § 2.	Hazakah 5:259-61
Agrarian Laws	Irur 5:587
1:124-26	Lease 6:578-80
Real Estate 9:92	Mortgage 7:657
Boundaries,	Four Cubits 4:363
Removal of 2:485	

9. Legal Documents

Documents, Legal	Attestation 1:608-9
3:583-84	Mamrem 7:308

10. Law of Representation

Agency, Legal	Trusts and Trustees
1:115-17	10:316-17
Attorney 1:609	Broker 2:544
Power of Attorney	Messenger 7:499
8:611-12	

11. Religious Law

Most of the subjects under religious law are treated under special heads, such as are found in the outlines on such topics as Judaism, Liturgy, Customs and Ceremonies, Ethics, Diet and Hygiene, or Costume. The following are of more general application:

Blasphemy 2:389	Mixtures, Prohibited
Vow 10:434-35	7:598-99
Work Prohibited on	Yayin Nesech 10:587
the Sabbath 10:573	Blood § 1. 2:406
Erub 4:158-59	

The following topics deal with legal discussions of modern times:

Birth Control	Head, Covering of
2:380-81	5:262-63
Athletics 1:583-84	Autopsy 1:642

For a general presentation of the spirit underlying Jewish law, see

Law, Spirit of the 6:561-64

OUTLINE 60:   JEWISH LAW.
C.   COURT PROCEDURE

The Jewish court system has a history of nearly three thousand years, reaching back to Bible times and continuing even today in the form of special voluntary Jewish Courts of Arbitration. This outline surveys the methods of procedure in courts developed under Jewish law.

The comprehensive article on the subject is

COURTS 3:385-89

Prior to the development of courts, justice in criminal cases was frequently carried out by the family, and it was only gradually that it became a public function. This is treated in the articles

Redeemer 9:97-98
Blood Revenge 2:410-12
Cities of Refuge 3:216

Jewish courts were of two kinds, those for criminal and those for civil cases. The criminal court was called

Sanhedrin 9:361-63

Civil cases were tried in arbitration panels of three, discussed in the articles

Arbitration 1:454-56   Beth Din 2:250

The general procedure in the trial of cases before Jewish courts is described in

Procedure at Law 8:649-50

Law, Criminal 6:554

The next group of articles deals with the details of the trial, which began with

Information 5:564

The participants in the trial were

Judge 6:258-60   Witnesses 10:549-50

Either might be disqualified as the result of

Suspicion 10:108   Bribery 2:525-26

The elements of the trial were one or more of

Admonition 1:98   Confession § 1. 3:328
Evidence 4:199   Oath 8:261-63
Proof 8:655

Evidence could be invalidated as a result of proof of

Alibi 1:184   Perjury 8:458

Jewish law differs from other law in the position given to

Appeal 1:433-34

In criminal cases, the verdict might be one of

Acquittal 1:74-75

In case of a conviction, punishment might be

Capital Punishment   Fines 4:305
3:25-27   Imprisonment 5:548
Corporal Punishment   Banishment 2:63-64
3:370-71

In civil cases, the court often asked the parties to consent to a

Compromise 3:323

In all such cases the verdict would indicate that one of the parties must hand over a piece of property or a sum of money to the other. In some cases, where the sum was not on hand, it was necessary to value the property of the loser of the case to see what he had to surrender in payment of his debt. For this the court was empowered to make an

Appraisement 1:435-36

See also the general legal principles enumerated in the outline 59, under *Civil* and *Criminal Law*.

OUTLINE 61: ANIMALS AND PLANTS

A description of the chief animals of Palestine is found in

FAUNA OF PALESTINE 4:256-64

Legal and literary references to animals in Jewish literature are given in

Animals 1:321-28

Other general topics pertaining to animals are

Animals, Protection of 1:330-31
Animals, Future Reward and Punishment of 1:330
Animals, Fabulous 1:328-29

The following animals are given individual articles:

Birds 2:367   Locust 7:152
Dove 3:592   Quail 9:44
Fish 4:318-19   Serpent 9:484
Lion 7:71-72

A description of the chief plants of Palestine is found in

FLORA OF PALESTINE 4:331-41

The following plants are given individual articles

Apple 1:435   Myrtle 8:73
Cedar 3:71   Thornbush 10:248
Myrrh 8:73

A discussion of mandrakes is found in the article

Aphrodisiacs 1:414-15

PART V: JEWS AND NON-JEWS

OUTLINE 62:

JUDAISM AND OTHER RELIGIONS

Judaism has again and again been compelled to meet the challenge of other religions with which its followers came into contact. In Bible times there was a long struggle before the religion of Israel could emerge from idolatry, and in the post-Biblical period new religions arose which claimed to be the logical successors of Judaism. Furthermore, both these and other religions interacted with Judaism, producing an exchange of ideas and customs, and, in modern times especially, working toward a common goal.

The articles in this field can be grouped as follows:

1. The Religions of Canaan

2. Religions of the Ancient World

3. Christianity 3:177-86

(*see* the separate outline on CHRISTIANITY)

4. Islam 5:610-13

5. Modern Religious Movements

OUTLINE 63: CHRISTIANITY

Judaism and Christianity bear an unusual relationship to one another. As has been frequently said, they are mother and daughter religions. Christianity is the product of certain ideas and aspirations in Judaism which developed in a direction outside of Judaism and to some extent under non-Jewish influence and thus ultimately led to a distinct cleavage between the two faiths. Accordingly, the student should have an idea of the development of Judaism up to the point when Christianity arose. This will be found in the outline on JEWISH HISTORY BY PERIODS, sections 1 through 7, and in the outlines on BIBLE, APOCRYPHA AND PSEUDEPIGRAPHA, RELIGION OF ISRAEL and JUDAISM. The following articles are of special value as background material:

A general view of the subject is given in

CHRISTIANITY 3:177-86

Since the main sources for the understanding of Christianity are its own literature, Jewish sources being practically non-existent, the Christian literature should be studied first, then the great Christian leaders, the doctrines and early sects, and finally the relationship between Judaism and Christianity.

Accordingly, the articles in this field fall into the following groups:

1. Christian Literature
New Testament 8:174-75
Gospels 5:68-69

2. Christian Leaders
Jesus of Nazareth 6:83-87

Paul 8:415-17

Church Fathers 3:203-4

Popes 8:587-99

3. Christian Sects

4. Christian Doctrines

5. Christian Rites and Institutions

6. Relations Between Christians and Jews

OUTLINE 64:

JEWS AS OBSERVED BY NON-JEWS

An interesting field of study is that of the opinions about Jews that have been recorded by non-Jews in the course of centuries of contact. These opinions are of all sorts—favorable, unfavorable or neutral—and in their sequence they afford a moving panorama of the culture of the Jews and their relations with their environment.

The literature on Jews in ancient times is described in

Greek Writers on Jews 5:93-95
Roman Writers on Jews 9:185-86

Special articles are given to
Cicero, Marcus Tullius 3:205 (Rome)
Apella 1:414 (Rome)
The literature on Jews in medieval and modern times is treated in

Christian Writers on Jews 3:175-76
Literature on and by Jews 7:100-25
American Literature on and by Jews § I.
1:259-62

The following individuals are given separate articles:

See also the indivdual names listed under ANTI-SEMITISM and PHILO-SEMITES.

OUTLINE 65:   ANTI-SEMITISM

The term anti-Semitism is used in this outline to include all manifestations of hatred and discrimination against the Jews in the course of history. Starting out as an antipathy to strangers, and persisting through the Middle Ages on a religious basis, it has been given a racial slant in modern times. But no matter what reasons it invokes, what charges it makes, what justifications it seeks, it remains the outstanding blot on modern civilization. The comprehensive article on the subject, with a history of developments up to 1939, is

ANTI-SEMITISM 1:341-409

Developments subsequent to 1939 are treated in the closing sections of the articles on various countries of Europe and Africa.

Other articles in this field may be grouped as follows:

1. Anti-Semitic Racial Theories

Aryanism 1:517-29   Nazism 8:135-37

answered by

Race, Jewish 9:60-62   Blood § 2. 2:406-7

2. Anti-Semitic Canards and Their Refutation

The comprehensive article on the subject is
 CANARDS 3:1-10

The principal subjects under this head are

a. **Blood Accusation 2:407-10**

  William of Norwich 10:522-23
  Hugh of Lincoln 5:478-79
  Simon of Trent 9:544
  Velizh Blood Accusation 10:400
  Damascus Affair 3:452
  Saratov Blood Accusation 9:369
  Tiszaeszlár Blood Accusation 10:253
  Xanten Blood Accusation 10:582
  Polna Trial 8:583
  Konitz Affair 6:448
  Beilis Case 2:139-41

b. **Host Desecration 5:471-72**

  Deggendorf 3:515

c. **Elders of Zion, Protocols of 4:46-60**

d. **Akkum 1:151**

e. **Relics, Desecration of 9:123-24**

f. **Criminality of Jews 3:416-22**

g. **Franklin, Benjamin 4:413-14**

h. **Lincoln, Abraham 7:68**

3. Attempts to Convert the Jews by Force

Baptism, Compulsory 2:68-69
Inquisition 5:566-70
Auto da Fé 1:640-41
Sermons, Compulsory 9:483-84

4. Attacks on Jewish Literature

Torah, Burning and Desecration of 10:269
Talmud, Burning and Desecration of 10:165
Confiscation of Hebrew Books 3:330-31
Censorship 3:80-83

5. Economic and Social Measures Against the Jews

Discriminatory Laws 3:568-69
Agriculture II, § 3. 1:126-27
Oath More Judaico 8:263
Repudiation of Debts 9:135-36
Jew Badge 6:89-90
Ghetto 4:597-603
Residence, Rights and Limitations of 9:137
Numerus Clausus 8:251-53
Boycott § 1. 2:486-89

6. Outbreaks of Violence

Crusades 3:427-29
Armleder 1:483
Black Death 2:386-87
Flagellants 4:322
Fettmilch Riot 4:282-83
Chmielnicki Massacres 3:161-62
Pogroms 8:559-62
Cemeteries, Desecration of 3:74
Synagogues, Burning and Desecration of 10:132-33

7. Incidents in which Anti-Semitism was an Important Factor

Keiley Case 6:356 (US)
Dreyfus Case 3:596-99 (F)
Bloom Incident 2:412 (US)
Frank, Leo, Case of 4:394-95 (US)
Rosenbluth Case 9:211-12 (US)

A special article is devoted to
Ku Klux Klan 6:479-82

8. Notorious Anti-Semites (in chronological order)

Manetho 7:321-22 (Egypt)
Apostomus 1:432-33 (P)
Apion 1:415 (Egypt)
Lampon 6:518 (Egypt)
Agobard of Lyon 1:120 (F)
Martin, Raymond 7:386 (S)
Rindfleisch 9:165 (G)
Ferrer, Vincente 4:280 (S, F)
Capistrano, Johann 3:24-25 (Po)
Spina, Alfonso de 10:4 (S)
Bernardino da Feltre 2:225 (I)
Eisenmenger, Johann Andreas 4:36-37 (G)
Rohling, August 9:182-83 (A)
Lagarde, Paul de 6:510 (G)
Drumont, Edouard Adolphe 3:603 (F)
Dühring, Eugen 3:607 (G)
Chamberlain, Houston Stewart 3:109 (G)
Petliura, Simon 8:471 (Ru)
Hauser, Otto 5:251-52 (G)
Hitler, Adolf 5:400-2 (G)

9. Defense Against Anti-Semitism.

Self-Defense Organizations 9:465-66
Boycott § II. 2:489-90
Better Understanding 2:257-70

Anti-Defamation League 1:336
Ligue pour le défense des droits de l'homme et
du citoyen 7:60-61
Non-Sectarian Anti-Nazi League 8:231-32
Verein zur Abwehr des Antisemitismus 10:405

OUTLINE 66: PHILO-SEMITES

The pages of Jewish history record many noble
names of those who championed the cause of the
oppressed Jews and aided them in securing freedom and justice. Their number increased in
modern times with the spread of the ideas of
democracy, liberty and equality.

The comprehensive article on the subject is

PHILO-SEMITES 8:497-99

The following individuals, arranged in chronological order, rendered particular services in behalf of the Jews:

Erasmus Desiderius 4:150 (Ho)
Reuchlin, Johann 9:145 (G)
Osiander, Andreas 8:333 (G)
Lessing, Gotthold Ephraim 6:613 (G)
Dohm, Christian Wilhelm von 3:586 (G)
Clermont-Tonnerre, Stanislas 3:220 (F)

Mirabeau, Honoré 7:578 (F)
Grégoire, Henri 5:100-1 (F)
Macaulay, Thomas Babington 7:259 (E)
Wergeland, Henrik Arnold 10:502-3 (N)
Brunetti, Angelo 2:566 (I)
Kossuth, Louis (Lajos) 6:459 (Hu)
Vance, Zebulon Baird 10:395 (US)
Mommsen, Theodor 7:616-17 (G)
Masaryk, Thomas G. 7:393-94 (Cz)
Korolenko, Vladimir 6:457 (Ru)
Clemenceau, Georges 3:219 (F)
Leroy-Beaulieu, Anatole de 6:611-12 (F)
Jaurès, Jean 6:46-47 (F)
Zola, Émile 10:671-72 (F)
Strack, Hermann 10:70-71 (G)
Abbott, Lyman 1:16-17 (US)
Gorki, Maxim 5:67 (Ru)
Kol, Henri Hubert van 6:441 (Ho)
Sterling, Ada 10:51 (US)
Van Paassen, Pierre 10:393 (US)
Parkes, James W. 8:402 (E)
Toscanini, Arturo 10:282 (US)

Assistance to the Jews on the part of governments
is described in

INTERVENTION 5:581-82

For this see also the articles
Damascus Affair 3:452
Beilis Case 2:139-41

PART VI: GENERAL SUBJECTS

OUTLINE 67: JEWISH ARCHEOLOGY

Jewish archeology covers the field of the exploration and interpretation of ancient objects and customs of Palestine and the neighboring countries, as well as the investigation of objects relating to specifically Jewish observances and customs.

The subject as a whole is discussed in

ARCHEOLOGY, JEWISH 1:459-66

The effect of the discoveries of archeology on the knowledge and interpretation of the Bible is treated in

Archeology and the Bible 1:457-59

General archeological topics are presented in the articles

Excavations 4:201-4	(illus. 1:105, 128,
Inscriptions 5:570	170, 173; 6:28;
Epigraphy 4:137	8:47)
Paleography 8:346	Dolmens 3:587
Assyriology 1:567-69	Caves 3:69-71
Sumerians 10:102	Catacombs, Jewish
Papyri 8:387	3:64-66
Ostraca 8:333-34	(illus. 5:629)
Ossuaries 8:333	Fortresses 4:359-60
Numismatics 8:253-56	

The articles listed below deal with specific archeological explorations and finds

Gezer 4:595-96	Shiloah (Siloam)
Ras Shamra	9:508
Inscriptions 9:77	Murashu Texts 8:42
Amarna Letters 1:221	Dura-Europos
Israel Stele 5:617-18	3:609-11
Megiddo 7:437-38	Beth Alpha 2:249-50
Moabite Stone 7:603	

There is additional archeological information in such articles as

Palestine 8:351-53,	Crete 3:410-12
355-57	Delos 3:519
Synagogue 10:120-22	Delphi 3:519-20
Corinth 3:369-70	

Among the biographical articles are those of the following archeologists:

Albright, William Foxwell 1:162-63 (US)
Speiser, Ephraim Avigdor 9:692 (US)
Krauss, Samuel 6:467-68 (Hu, E)
Dalman, Gustaf 3:448 (G)
Klein, Samuel 6:415-16 (Hu, P)
Löw, Immanuel 7:213-14 (Hu)
Sukenik, Eleazar Lipa 10:94 (P)
Chipiez, Charles 3:160 (F)
Glueck, Nelson 4:627 (US)
Gordon, Cyrus Herzl 5:61 (US)
Kitchener of Khartoum, Lord Horatio Herbert 6:408 (E)

Macalister, Robert 7:258-59 (E)
Wischnitzer-Bernstein, Rachel 10:532 (G, US)
The following organization is devoted to archeological exploration in Palestine:
Palestine Exploration Fund 8:375

OUTLINE 68: SYMBOLS

Symbols serve the purpose of providing a definite and tangible object upon which to center an idea or a loyalty. In the course of history various objects have been given a symbolic meaning in Judaism and have become favorite themes for decoration and ornamentation or have furnished favorite figures of speech in literature.

The general article on the subject is

SYMBOLS AND SYMBOLISM 10:118-19

Details are found under the following heads:

1. Symbolic Interpretation

Bride 2:527-28	Horn 5:454-55
King and Kingdom	Fire 4:310-11
6:384-86	Light 7:59
Crown 3:426	

2. Symbolic Objects

Banners 2:66
Menorah 7:487-90
Commandments, The Ten 3:314-15
Shield of David 9:506-7
Swastika 10:111 (illus. 1:519)

See also the outlines on ART AND ARCHITECTURE, SYNAGOGUE, and CUSTOMS AND CEREMONIES.

OUTLINE 69: FOLKLORE

Mysticism and folklore have much in common. The first is the attempt of the intellectuals to understand and control the mysteries of the universe; the second is a similar attempt on the part of the common man. Both have furnished aid to the human soul when confronted with subjects too great for immediate comprehension. Folklore is more primitive, more naïve, and tends to disappear with the coming of greater knowledge and understanding of the universe through the achievements of science.

A general outline of the subject is given in the article

FOLKLORE 4:348-49

Other articles in this field may be grouped as follows:

1. The Folklore of the Bible

Mythology 8:76-77   Gilgamesh 4:610-11

2. Attempts to Ascertain the Future

Divination 3:575
Necromancy 8:140-41
Astrology 1:570-71
Bibliomancy 2:348-49
Nostradamus 8:245-46

3. MAGIC 7:273-75

Witchcraft 10:548-49
Magic Squares 7:275
Baal Shem 2:3
Falk, Hayim Samuel
4:237

4. SUPERSTITION 10:103-4

Demons 3:529-34
Exorcism 4:215
Dreams 3:593-95
Evil Eye 4:199-200
Amulets 1:288-91
Abracadabra
1:34-35
Abraxas 1:55
Dybbuk 3:615

5. Fabulous Animals

Animals, Fabulous
1:328-29
Rahab 9:67
Behemoth 2:137
Leviathan 6:628
Shamir 9:494-95

6. LEGENDS 6:590-91

Elijah § 2. 4:75
Messiah 7:499-503
Lost Tribes 7:203-5
Tribes, Ten Lost
10:304-5
Bene Mosheh 2:165
Sambation 9:339
Water of Life 10:475
Africa § 2. Folklore
1:109-10
Shetiah 9:505
Alexander the Great
§ 2. In Jewish
Literature 1:172
Antoninus 1:412-13
Bar Shalmon 2:75
Bar Temalion 2:75-76
Luz §§ 2. and 3.
7:244
Andreas 1:301-2
Amram of Mayence
1:283
Amnon of Mayence
1:277
Golem 5:43-46
Lamed Vav Zaddikim
6:512-13
Prochownik, Abraham
8:651-52
Wahl, Saul 10:440

7. Legends of Jewish Content but Non-Jewish Origin

Wandering Jew 10:448-49
Anglo-Israelism 1:316-17

8. Ceremonies in Which There is a Folklore Basis

Birth 2:379-80
Holle Kreish 5:443
Tashlich 10:177
Kappores 6:313
Wedding and Wedding
Customs 10:480-82
Burial and Burial
Customs 2:594-602

OUTLINE 70:

FAMILIES AND FAMILY TREES

Many of the articles in the encyclopedia deal with family groups, tracing their origin, relationship and descent. This subject is treated generally in the article

GENEALOGY 4:526-27

Jewish families which have been raised to the nobility are discussed in

Nobility 8:230-31
Coats of Arms 3:225-28 (illus. 1:53; 2:106, 5:15)

Modern associations based on families are described in

Family Circles 4:244

The following articles deal with families and family names. An asterisk (*) indicates that the article gives the derivation or history of the name in question:

Abendana 1:21
Abravanel 1:53
Abudiente 1:60
*Abulafia 1:60
*Adler 1:85
Alatrini 1:156
*Alfakar 1:176
Alfandari 1:177
Algazi 1:180
*Altschul 1:215-16
Amarillo 1:221
*Anav 1:297
Arnstein, von 1:485
*Ashkenazi 1:543
*Astruc 1:576
*Athias 1:580-81
*Auerbach 1:611
*Bacharach 2:19
*Bagi 2:31
Bak 2:36
Bakri 2:38
Baneth 2:63
*Bardach 2:84
*Basilea 2:104
Belmont 2:152-53
*Belmonte 2:153-54
*Benveniste 2:187
*Bettelheim 2:256
*Bing 2:354-5
*Bischoffsheim 2:383
*Bloch 2:394-95
Bloomingdale 2:414-15
*Bondi 2:450
Boton 2:484
Brentano 2:520-21
Brodsky 2:540
Bueno 2:579-80
*Caceres, de 2:621
Calahora 2:629
Calmer 2:647
*Carmona 3:48-49
Carvalho 3:54-55
Note—Solomon
Solis Carvalho
d.1942
Cases (Cazes) 3:55
*Castro, de 3:61
Cattaui 3:67-68
Note—Joseph
Cattaui Pasha
d.1942
*Chajes 3:107
*Cohen 3:233
Cohen (of Baltimore)
3:233-36
Cohen (of England)
3:236
Cone 3:325-26
Coriat 3:369
Costa, da 3:373
*Covo 3:390
David 3:485
Dawidsohn 3:492-93
De Sola 3:500-1
*Eger 4:3
*Eibenschitz 4:21
*Ephraim 4:135-36
*Epstein 4:140
*Errera 4:155
Etting 4:186-90
*Ezra 4:227-28
Falk 4:236-37
Farjeon 4:248
*Finzi 4:309-10
Fischel 4:315-16
Flexner 4:326
*Foa 4:345
Fonseca 4:355
Frankau 4:397
Franklin 4:412-13
Franks 4:416-18
Freiberg 4:434-35
*Friedenwald 4:447-49
*Galante 4:492
*Gatigno 4:518
Gentili 4:534-35
Gimbel 4:611
*Goitein 5:11
Goldschmidt-
Rothschild 5:33
Goldsmid 5:33-35
Gomez 5:49-50

GENEALOGY—*Continued*

For additional information on the origin of Jewish family names, see

---

OUTLINE 71: MESSIAH AND
MESSIANIC MOVEMENTS

The idea of a Messiah as the deliverer of Israel from oppression and degradation arose gradually in Judaism and was the combination of several ideas which coalesced around a single figure. As a doctrine it was never fixed or definite; it pointed to a better future, but the exact terms of that future fluctuated with the thought of the time. The Messianic hope was almost forgotten in periods of prosperity; in times of persecution, however, it grew in power, and formed the vehicle for numerous pretenders to Messiahship to assert their claims and to win followers.

In order to understand the background of the Messiah ideal, it is best to read the articles

The idea of a ruling dynasty was then connected with ideas of

As a result of this fusion there arose the hope expressed in the belief in

MESSIAH 7:499-503

MESSIANIC ERA 7:503-4

The idea of a specially appointed opponent of the Messiah appears in

The belief in the Messiah led the Jews into various

MESSIANIC MOVEMENTS 7:505-6

Of these, that of Christianity is treated in a special outline.

Later Messianic claimants or visionaries were, in chronological order,

Bar Kochba 2:72
Isfahani, Abu Isa 5:607
Yudghan 10:617
Alroy, David 1:206-7
Abulafia, Abraham ben Samuel 1:60-62
Lemmlein, Asher 6:604
Molcho, Solomon 7:613-14
    (see also Reubeni, David 9:144-45)
Luria, Isaac 7:237-39
Sabbatai Zevi 9:292-95
    Ghazzati, Nathan 4:596-97
    Dönmeh 3:590
Cardoso, Abraham Miguel 3:38
Prossnitz, Löbele 9:4

An aftermath of the Messianic movements and the disappointment engendered by them was the notorious

Frank, Jacob Leibovicz, and the Frankist Movement 4:390-93

OUTLINE 72:

POLITICAL AND SOCIAL MOVEMENTS

The purpose of this outline is to show how the Jews reacted to the various political and social movements in the course of their history. Contrary to common belief, they have never tended to follow any individual political party, although they have always been attracted to those movements which held out a promise of freedom and equality. There have been Jewish leaders in movements of the most opposite tendencies, and on the whole Jews have tended to divide among various political and social groups in the same ratios as their non-Jewish neighbors of similar social and economic status.

The various movements are arranged in the order in which Jews began to participate in them. As far back as Bible times they were practising

Democracy 3:522-28

In the same period and for many centuries after some Jews believed in

Asceticism 1:532-33

Movements which were connected with their occupations were

Internationalism 5:579-81
Capitalism, Role of Jews in 3:28-34

The struggle for liberty is reflected in

Masonry 7:397-99
Religious Liberty 9:128-31

Christian State, Doctrine of 3:174
Church and State 3:196-201
Bible in Public Schools 2:327-28

Anti-Slavery Movement and the Jews 1:410

Brown, John, Jewish Associates of 2:563
The first of the modern social reform movements was

Socialism 9:583-86

The most important Jewish Socialist organizations are

Bund 2:587-89   Hapoel Hatzair
Poale Zion 8:554-55   5:212-13

The most important Jewish Socialist leaders, arranged in chronological order, were or are

Lassalle, Ferdinand 6:542-44 (G)
Adler, Victor 1:97 (A)
Singer, Paul 9:557 (G)
Meissner, Alfred 7:448 (Cz)
Winter, Lev (Leo) 10:530-31 (Cz, A)
Abramowitz, Raphael 1:52 (Ru)
Bauer, Otto 2:114-15 (A)
Berger, Victor L. 2:199-200 (US)
Bernstein, Eduard 2:234 (G)
Hillquit, Morris 5:369-70 (US)
London, Meyer 7:184-86 (US)
Toller, Ernst 10:263-64 (G)

The second of the modern social reform movements was

Anarchism 1:294

The following are the only Jewish anarchist leaders of importance:

Berkman, Alexander 2:203-4 (US)
Goldman, Emma 5:23-24 (US)
Mühsam, Ehrich 8:32 (G)

Movements which have affected the Jews from 1880 to the present day are

Labor Movement and the Jews 6:504-5

(for details, see the outline on LABOR AND LABOR ORGANIZATIONS)

Nationalism, Jewish 8:126-32
Pacifism 8:341-42
Communism 3:315-20

The following are the most important Jewish Communists, arranged in chronological order:

Marx, Karl 7:389-90 (G, E)
Zinoviev, Grigorii 10:644-45 (Ru)
Kamenev, Leo 6:302 (Ru)
Trotsky, Leon D. 10:312-13 (Ru)
Radek, Karl 9:64 (Ru)
Litvinoff, Maxim 7:143-45 (Ru)
Luxemburg, Rosa 7:243 (G)
Leviné, Eugene 6:632-33 (G)
Kun, Béla 6:486-87 (Hu, Ru)
Kaganovich, Lazar 6:279 (Ru)
Neumann, Heinz 8:159 (G)
Borodin, Michael 2:477-78 (Ru, China)
Sverdlov, Iakov M. 10:110-11 (Ru)

The latest movement to win Jewish followers is

Cooperatives 3:353-63

OUTLINE 73:

LABOR AND LABOR ORGANIZATIONS

The just and equitable treatment of labor was one of the earliest interests of Jewish law. Beginning with the legislation of the Bible, a series of laws provided for a fair and proper treatment of the laboring man. During the Middle Ages Jews joined in labor organizations of their own, and in modern times they have contributed to the weight and effectiveness of the labor movement.

The general articles on the subject are

LABOR 6:497-504

LABOR MOVEMENT AND THE JEWS 6:504-5

Jewish labor organizations of former times are treated under

Guilds, Jewish 5:124-27

The most important Jewish labor leaders, arranged in chronological order, are

Gompers, Samuel 5:50-52 (US)
De Leon, Daniel 3:498 (US)
Stokes, Rose Pastor 10:67 (US)
Schlossberg, Joseph 9:411 (US)
Kaplansky, Solomon 6:311 (P)
Schneiderman, Rose 9:413 (US)
Ben Gurion, David 2:158-59 (P)
Vladeck, B. Charney 10:429-30 (US)
Dubinsky, David 3:604-5 (US)
Hillman, Sidney 5:368-69 (US)
Kaznelson, Berl 6:350 (P)

The general articles on Jewish labor unions in modern times are

Trade Unions 10:286-90
Artisans § VI. 1:515

The following are the organizations in which Jewish labor has played an important role:

Amalgamated Clothing Workers of America 1:218-20
Hapoel Hamizrahi 5:212
Hapoel Hatzair 5:212-13
Histadruth Haobedim 5:384-85
International Ladies' Garment Workers' Union 5:578-79
International Workers Order 5:579
Jewish Labor Committee 6:133
Poale Zion 8:554-55
Poalei Agudath Israel 8:555-56
Workmen's Circle 10:574

OUTLINE 74: ZIONISM

Zionism is the most active Jewish movement of the 20th century. Starting among small groups in the 1880's, it acquired a definite form and organization through the efforts of Theodor Herzl. It attained its first end with the issuing of the Balfour Declaration in 1917, and since the first World War has devoted itself to the rehabilitation of Palestine.

The comprehensive article on the subject is

ZIONISM 10:645-67

Articles dealing with various subordinate topics are

Basel Program 2:103
Zionist Congresses 10:668 (for pictures of the delegates to the First Zionist Congress, see opposite 2:102)
Hatikvah 5:249
Balfour Declaration 2:45-49
Palestine Mandate 8:376-78

Movements closely allied to Zionism are

Territorialism 10:200-1
    Angola 1:318-19
    Zangwill, Israel 10:627-29 (E)
Nationalism, Jewish 8:126-32

The chief Zionist leaders, arranged in the approximate order of their rise to prominence in the movement, were or are

Hess, Moses 5:344-45 (for the ideology) (G, F)
Pinsker, Leo 8:537-38 (Ru)
Schapira, Hermann 9:389-90 (Ru, G)
Ahad Haam 1:135-36 (Ru, P)
Birnbaum, Nathan 2:369-70 (A, Ho)
Motzkin, Leo 8:23-24 (Ru, G, F)
Herzl, Theodor 5:337-43 (A)
Nordau, Max 8:233-36 (Hu, F)
Levin, Shemarya 6:632 (Ru, G, US, P)
De Haas, Jacob 3:497 (E, US)
Ussishkin, Menahem Mendel 10:384-85 (Ru, P)
Goldberg, Abraham (d. 1942) 5:12-13 (US)
Wolffsohn, David 10:558-59 (G)
Sokolow, Nahum 9:590-92 (Po, G, E)
Weizmann, Chaim 10:495-99 (Ru, Swi, E)
Wise, Stephen Samuel 10:543-44 (US)
Lipsky, Louis 7:79-80 (US)
Szold, Henrietta 10:147-48 (US, P)
Brandeis, Louis Dembitz (d. 1941) 2:495-99 (US)
Mack, Julian William 7:266 (US)

The leader of the Zionist Revisionists, or New Zionist group, was

Jabotinsky, Vladimir 6:2-4 (Ru, P, G, E, US)

The chief financial and administrative agencies of the Zionist Organization are

Jewish Colonial Trust, Limited, The 6:96 (E)
Anglo-Palestine Bank Ltd., The 1:318 (E, P)
Jewish National Fund 6:134-38 (P)
Palestine Foundation Fund 8:375-76 (US)
Jewish Agency for Palestine 6:91-93 (P)

The following articles deal with Zionist organizations:

Avukah 1:649-50
Berith Shalom 2:203
Brith Trumpeldor 2:534
Hadassah 5:147-50
Hashomer Hatzair 5:236-37

Histadruth Haobedim 5:384-85
  Hapoel Hatzair 5:212
  Poale Zion 8:554-55
Irgun Tzebai Leumi 5:586
Mizrachi 7:599-600
Order Sons of Zion 8:318
Women's International Zionist Organization
  10:569
Young Judaea 10:607-8

OUTLINE 75:
RACE, NATION OR RELIGION?

One of the most intricate and actively discussed
questions about the Jews is whether they constitute a race, a nation or a religion. The problem is further complicated by the fact that both
race and nation are indefinite terms, and that, in
reference to religion, Jews who have abandoned
the Jewish religion are still regarded as belonging
to the Jewish people. The encyclopedia, as the
representative of all of Jewry, has endeavored to
present all sides of this issue, in order that the
reader may judge for himself and draw his own
conclusions.

The articles dealing with the question of race
are

RACE, JEWISH 9:60-62

Types, Jewish 10:330-32
Blood § 2. 2:406-7
Additional sidelights are found in
  Semites 9:473-74   Aryanism 1:517-29
The two main divisions of the Jewish people are
treated in
  Ashkenaz and Ashkenazim 1:541-43
  Sephardim 9:477-78
Smaller groups of various racial or national
origins are
  Daggatuns 3:446   Krimchaki 6:471
  Falashas 4:234-36   Mountain Jews
  Negro Jews 8:145   8:25-28
  Khazars 6:375-78   Beni Israel 2:173-76
The pros and cons of Jewish nationalism are pre-
sented in

NATIONALISM, JEWISH 8:126-32

The religious view of the Jewish people is set
forth in the articles

CHOSEN PEOPLE 3:164-69
MISSION OF ISRAEL 7:582-84

The bearing of this question of race, nation or
religion on Jewish attitudes in present day life
is discussed in
  Assimilation 1:556-61
  Jewish Question 6:140-41

OUTLINE 76:
FACTS AND FIGURES ABOUT JEWS

This outline is devoted to presenting those
articles which furnish a quick and ready reference to information about Jews in general, thus
answering numerous questions which arise in the
course of reading and study about Jews and
Judaism.

The following articles contain statistical information about Jews:

STATISTICS 10:23-36

Health of the Jews 5:263-68
Criminality of Jews 3:416-22
Migrations of the Jews 7:543-56
Refugees 9:103-10
Difficulties in the past gathering of information
are discussed in
  Census 3:83
The following articles deal with the losses from
and gains to the number of the Jews by reason of
conversion to other religions and accession of
proselytes to Judaism:

CONVERTS 3:341-46

Apostates 1:427-31   Chuetas 3:194
Marranos 7:366-69   Judaizers 6:246-48

PROSELYTES 9:1-3

Pacradounis 8:342   Beni Israel 2:173-76
Khazars 6:375-78   Falashas 4:234-36
Krimchaki 6:471

A phenomenon which may operate in either direction is

Mixed Marriage 7:593-98

The chief article dealing with the occupations
followed by Jews is

OCCUPATIONS 8:265-79

The following are some of the occupations, arranged approximately in the order in which they
were entered by Jews:

Shepherd 9:503   Dye Industry, Jews in
Agriculture § 1.   3:615-16
  1:121-24   Money Lending
Artisans 1:501-15   7:618-22
Handicrafts 5:201-4   Minters 7:577
Tax Collectors   Diamond Trade,
  10:179-80   Jews in 3:558-59
Slave Trade 9:565-66   Needle Trades
                         8:141-44

In addition to these, consult the outlines on Jews
in FINANCE, ART, MUSIC, and the various pro-
fessions and scientific fields.

Modern Jewish agriculture is discussed in
  Colonies, Agricultural 3:268-303

The formation of a Jewish working class is treated in

Proletariat, Jewish 8:654-55

The various names by which the Jews have been called are

Hebrews 5:287
Israelites 5:620
Jew 6:89

Jeshurun 6:81
People of the Book
8:434

Class divisions of Jews created by the religious law are treated in

CASTES 3:60

Priestly Caste
8:635-37
Levites 7:1-4

Nethinim 8:152-53
Laymen 6:566

The following articles are of general interest:

Names of the Jews 8:90-98
Jewish Culture 6:126-28
Jewish Question 6:140-41
Caricature, Jew in 3:43-47
Civilization 3:217-18
Nobel Prize Winners, Jewish 8:228-29

See also the articles listed under the outline on RACE, NATION OR RELIGION.

PART VII: JEWISH CONTRIBUTIONS TO CIVILIZATION

The remaining outlines in this book are devoted to groupings of the biographies of individual Jews who have made notable contributions to the science, culture and institutions of modern life. Twenty-two outlines are devoted to specific fields in which Jews have been especially prominent; the last two outlines contain groupings of various fields which are worthy of notice, although too small to be given a separate outline.

It will be noticed that nearly all these biographies are those of Jews who lived in modern times. This is but natural. It was only in modern times that Jews have had the opportunity to exercise their talents in fields of free competition, unhampered by the many restrictions to which they had been subjected. Again, it is only in modern times that many of the fields mentioned in this section have reached a worthwhile development.

It is suggested that the reader of these outlines should first read some of the general articles in outline 76, especially those on Statistics 10:23-26, Migrations of the Jews 7:543-56, and Occupations 8:265-79, by way of a general background, in order to place in its proper perspective the particular field in which he is interested.

OUTLINE 77:

JEWS IN ART AND ARCHITECTURE

Art was slow to develop among the Jews because of the prohibition, in the Second Commandment, against the making of idols, which was interpreted as forbidding human representation in painting and sculpture. Paintings of human figures appeared only in synagogues outside of Palestine and later gradually disappeared. Jewish artists displayed skill in creating ceremonial objects for the home or the synagogue. It was only in modern times that Jews began to participate in more general artistic endeavor. Since the 19th century there have been numerous Jewish artists of reputation in every field of art. They have followed those modes of art which accorded with their own individual tastes, and by no means constitute a special type or school.

(Illustrations of the work of Jewish artists appear throughout the volumes of the encyclopedia. They are indicated by the volume and page indications given in parentheses.)

The comprehensive article on the subject is

ART, JEWS IN 1:489-500

The attitude of the Jews toward art is indicated in the article

Beauty 2:125-27

The following articles deal with various Jewish art objects from the earliest times:

Dura-Europos 3:609-11 (1:3, 461; 8:4)

Illumination of Manuscripts 5:539-42 (frontispiece, vol. 1; after 2:280; 4:548; frontispiece, vol. 5; 5:462, 591; 6:10; 7:289, 341)

Haggadah, Passover § 2. 5:157-64 (1:38, 79, 304, 453, 491, 493; 2:39, 479, after 516; 3:314, 473, before 629; 4:14; 5:184, 263, 421; frontispiece, vol. 6; 6:177; 7:335, 502; 8:409, 550)

Kethubah 6:367-72

Frescoes and Murals 4:438-41 (frontispiece, vol. 4)

Almemar 1:193

Ark (in the synagogue) 1:475-77 (1:232, 492; 2:653; 8:481, 483)

Parocheth 8:403

Torah, Ornamentation of 10:269-73 (3:98; 5:424; 7:148; 8:326)

Menorah 7:487-90 (1:623; 3:100; 4:374; 6:516-17)

Habdalah 5:140-43

Spiceboxes 10:1

Ablutions 1:24-26

Lamp 6:516-18 (1:519; 5:210-11; 7:60, 437)

Ring 9:165-66

Tombstones 10:265-67 (2:566; 3:106, 364; 4:4, 38, 139, 545; 5:487, 639-40; 6:314; 7:147, 250, 312, 444, 524; 8:240)

Collections of Jewish art objects are to be found in Museums 8:44-46

The most important of the numerous Jewish artists, in chronological order, are

Marlibrun 7:363-64 (E)

Ercole de'Fideli 4:150 (I)

Italia, Shalom 5:625 (Ho)

Cooper, Samuel 3:353 (E)

Cooper, (Abraham) Alexander 3:352 (E)

Mengs, Anton Raphael 7:484-85 (G, S, I)

Treu, Marquart 10:303 (G)

Zoffany, John 10:669-70 (G, E)

Oppenheim, Moritz Daniel 8:306-7 (G; 2:73, 392; 3:103; 4:560-61; 9:41, 454, 542)

Guttmann, Jakob 5:135-36 (Hu, A, F)

Bendemann, Eduard Julius Friedrich 2:163 (G; 2:13, 15)

Engel, József 4:109 (Hu, E, I)

Bonheur, Rosa 2:453-54 (F)

Pissarro, Camille 8:543-44 (F)

Israels, Jozef 5:621 (Ho; 2:312; 6:380)

Antokolski, Mark M. 1:411-12 (Ru; for his tombstone, see 9:283)

Rosenthal 9:217-18 (US)

Beer, Samuel Friedrich 2:135 (F)

Blum, Robert Frederic 2:418 (US)

Ezekiel, Sir Moses Jacob 4:224-25 (US)

Mosler, Henry 8:17-18 (US)

Levitan, Isaac Ilyitch 7:1 (Ru)

Rosenthal, Toby Eduard 9:222 (US, G)

Kaufmann, Isidor 6:344 (A; 9:297; vol. 10, color plate in article SUKKAH)

Cohen, Katherine M. 3:249 (US)

Loeb, Louis 7:156 (US)

Liebermann, Max 7:53-54 (G; 2:321)

Solomon, Solomon Joseph 9:642 (E; 9:342)

Keyser, Ephraim 6:373-74 (US)

Ury, Lesser 10:382-83 (G, F; 1:101; 2:309; 4:331; 6:8, 61)

Bakst, Leon 2:38-40 (Ru, F; 4:182)

Brenner, Victor David 2:520 (US)

Schatz, Boris 9:391-93 (F, Bu, P; 3:96; 6:273; 7:412; 8:664; 9:515)

Lilien, Ephraim Moses 7:61 (G; 1:308-9, 494, 505, 512; 9:36, 296; 10:578)

Fényes, Adolf 4:274 (Hu)

Pilichowski, Leopold 8:531-32 (Po, F, E; 1:72; 4:503)

Modigliani, Amedeo 7:606-7 (F)

Mielziner, Leo 7:541-42 (US)

Pissarro, Lucien 8:544 (F, E)

László, Philip Alexius 6:547 (Hu, E)

Sterner, Albert Edward 10:61-62 (US)

Iványi-Grünwald, Béla 5:643-44 (Hu)

Peixotto, Ernest Clifford 8:423-24 (US)

Nussbaum, Jacob 8:259 (G, P)

Halpert, Samuel 5:187 (US)

Glicenstein, Enrico 4:619-20 (I, US; 1:499; 2:71, 126; 7:500; 8:663; 10:5)

Ligeti, Miklós 7:59 (Hu)

Butensky, Jules Leon 2:608 (F, US; 1:214; 4:503)

Aronson, Naoum 1:488 (Ru, F)

Ries, Teresa Feodorowna 9:162 (Ru, A)

Struck, Hermann 10:87 (G; 1:504, 506; 10:592)

Veit, Philipp 10:399-400 (G)

Sterne, Maurice 10:61 (US, I; 7:405)

Raskin, Saul 9:80-81 (US; 4:179)

Ballin, Hugo 2:51 (US; 4:439; 7:199)

Epstein, Jacob 4:143-45 (E)

Weber, Max 10:479-80 (US)

Pann, Abel 8:383-84 (F, P)

Manievich, Abraham A. (d. 1942) 7:322-23 (Ru, US)

Davidson, Jo 3:489-90 (US; 1:496)

Kroll, Leon 6:475-76 (US)

Meidner, Ludwig 7:441-42 (G, E; 5:205)

Budko, Joseph 2:579 (G, P)

Oppenheimer, Max 8:312-13 (G, A, US)

Nadelman, Eli 8:81-82 (US)

Chagall, Marc 3:107 (F, Ru; 2:289)

Steinhardt, Jacob 10:46 (G, P; 6:8)

Zorach, William 10:673-74 (US)

Wolff, Gustav 10:552-53 (G, US)

Gertler, Mark 4:593 (E)

Rosenthal, Louis 9:220-21 (US; 1:495)

Orloff, Chana 8:325 (F)

Altmann, Nathan 1:212-13 (Ru)

Auerbach-Levy, William 1:612-13 (US; 4:503)

Zadkine, Ossip 10:624-25 (F, US)

Kisling, Maurice 6:404-5 (F, US)

Schotz, Benno 9:425 (Sc)

Lipchitz, Jacques 7:72 (F)

Kalish, Max 6:296 (US)

Zack, Léon 10:622 (Ru, G, F)

Rubin, Reuben 9:270 (P)

Paeff, Bashka 8:343-44 (US)

Szyk, Arthur 10:151 (Po, US; after 4:168; after 8:474; dedication page, vol. 10)

Moholy-Nagy, Ladislaus 7:611 (G, US)

Katz, Alexander Raymond 6:335-36 (US)

Margulies, Joseph 7:355-56 (US; 10:187)

Brackman, Robert 2:490 (US)

Grossman, Elias Mandel 5:106 (US; 5:95, 343; 6:2; 10:387, 590, 607)

Band, Max 2:62 (F, US)

Belskie, Abram 2:155 (US)

Of special interest are the Jewish connections of Rivera, Diego 9:172-73 (M)

Until the 19th century Jews did not enter the general field of architecture. Their sole efforts in that direction were devoted to the construction of synagogues. The general principles of synagogal architecture are treated in

ARCHITECTURE 1:466-67

Further details are given in

Synagogue § 4. 10:120-24 (with numerous illustrations)

The most important Jewish architects, in chronological order, are

Basevi, Joshua George 2:103 (E)

Rosengarten, Albrecht 9:214 (G)

Fernbach, Henry 4:279 (US)

Aldrophe, Alfred Philibert 1:166 (F)

Eidlitz, Leopold 4:22 (US)

Wechselman, Ignac Ritter von 10:480 (G, A, Hu)

Hirsch, Abraham 5:373 (F)

Adler, Dankmar 1:89 (US)

Messel, Alfred 7:498-99 (G)

Quittner, Zsigmond 9:46 (Hu)

Brunner, Arnold William 2:566-67 (US)

Joseph, Delissa 6:195 (E)

Sachs, Edwin O. 9:303 (E)

Alschuler, Alfred Samuel (d. 1939) 1:210 (US)

Jacobs, Harry Allan 6:17 (US)

Klerk, Michel de 6:417-18 (Ho)

Pontremoli, Emmanuel 8:586 (F)

Kahn, Albert 6:285-86 (d. 1942) (US)

Strnad, Oscar 10:85 86 (A)

Bálint, Zoltán 2:50 (Hu)

Nachtlicht, Leo 8:81 (A, G, US)

Kaufmann, Oskar 6:344 (G)

Meyers, Charles B. 7:522 (US)

Freedlander, Joseph H. 4:432 (US)

Wlach, Oscar 10:550-51 (A, I, T)

Sternfeld, Harry 10:62 (US)

Kahn, Ely Jacques 6:287 (US)

Mendelsohn, Erich 7:468-69 (G, E, P)

Jofan (Iofan), Boris Mikhailovich 6:162 (Ru)

Grunsfeld, Ernest Alton, Jr. 5:113 (US)

OUTLINE 78: JEWS IN ASTRONOMY

Jews began to take an interest in astronomy at least as early as the Talmudic period, when certain rabbis observed the phases of the moon and the courses of the stars in order to serve as experts on the calculation of the Jewish calendar and the proclamation of the new moon. During the Middle Ages Jewish scholars kept abreast of the secular knowledge of the time. In modern times, however, Jewish individuals began to make special contributions in all fields of astronomical science.

The general article on the subject is

ASTRONOMY 1:571-76

The following medieval Jewish writers dealt especially with astronomy:

Gans, David ben Solomon 4:511 (A)
Delmedigo, Joseph Solomon 3:518-19
  (Gr, I, G, A)

Jews in modern times who furthered the science of astronomy include

Herschel, Sir William 5:329 (E)
Herschel, Caroline Lucretia 5:329 (E)
Beer, Wilhelm 2:135 (G)
Rubenson, Robert 9:269 (Sw)
Abelman, Ilya Solomonovich 1:20 (Ru)
Löw, Moritz 7:215 (G)
Loewy, Maurice 7:166-67 (A, F)
Goldschmidt, Hermann 5:29 (F)
Oppenheim, Samuel 8:308 (A)
Cohn, Fritz 3:259-60 (G)
Cohn, Berthold 3:258 (G, F)
Israel, Edward 5:618 (US)
Schuster, Arthur 9:431 (E)
Schlesinger, Frank (d. 1943) 9:408 (US)
Bemporad, Azeglio 2:156 (I)
Marcuse, Adolf 7:350 (G)
Epstein, Paul Sophus 4:147-48 (Ru, US)
Berman, Louis 2:221 (US)
Michelson, Albert Abraham 7:532-34 (US)
Einstein, Albert 4:29-33 (G, Swi, US)

OUTLINE 79: JEWS IN ATHLETICS

Athletic exercises and games were a favorite diversion of the Jews in ancient times. The crowded conditions of the ghetto in the Middle Ages compelled Jews to relinquish sports, but as soon as an opportunity was afforded them with the growth of toleration, athletics revived among them.

The general article on the subject is

ATHLETICS 1:581-99

The following English Jewish boxers played a part in changing the attitude of the British public toward the Jews, thus facilitating Jewish emancipation:

Mendoza, Daniel 7:482-83
Belasco, Abraham 2:145
Belasco, Israel 2:147
Aaron, Barney 1:7

The following Jews won world championships in their respective classes as prizefighters:

Attell, Abe 1:608 (US)
Leonard, Benny 6:610 (US)
Ross, Barney 9:229 (US)
Baer, Max Adelbert 2:29 (US)

Jews who won distinction in other fields of athletics were

Copeland, Lillian 3:364 (US)
Abrahams, Harold Maurice 1:47 (E)
Abrahams, Sidney Solomon 1:49 (E)
Holman, Nat 5:444 (US)

The following, though not athletes, are of interest because of their connection with baseball:

Dreyfuss, Barney 3:600 (US)
Elias, Alfred Munro 4:67-68 (US)

The following are Jewish athletic associations:

Bar-Kochba Associations 2:72-73
Hapoel 5:212
Maccabi 7:264

OUTLINE 80: JEWS IN AVIATION

Jews began to participate in aviation almost from the moment that it began. While it is true that modern research has established the fact that the pioneer aviator, Otto Lilienthal, stated to be Jewish, was actually not a Jew, there were many Jews who made their contributions as inventors, patrons, engineers and pioneer fliers.

The introductory article on the subject is

AVIATION, JEWS IN 1:644-47
(*see also* the illustration in 2:378)

There are separate biographical articles on
Schwarz, David 9:435 (A, Ru)
Deutsch de la Meurthe, Henri 3:556 (F)
Walden, Henry W. 10:443-44 (US)
Rumpler, Eduard 9:276 (G)
Guggenheim, Daniel 5:119-20 (US)
Guggenheim, Harry 5:122-23 (US)
Arnstein, Karl 1:486 (G, US)
Kronfeld, Robert 6:477 (G, E)
Lipsner, Benjamin Berl 7:80 (US)
Bernstein, Lena 2:236-37 (F)
Kármán, Theodor von 6:325 (G, F, US)
Sassoon, (Ellice) Victor 9:378-79 (E)
Bernson, Edith Jane 2:232 (US)
Smushkevich, Iakov Vladimirovich 9:575-76
  (Ru)

Further information on Jews in military aviation is found in

Soldier, Jews as, beginning 9:604

OUTLINE 81: JEWS IN BIOLOGY

Biology began to develop as a separate science about the middle of the 19th century. Jews have participated in it from its beginnings, and have throughout contributed a notable number of leaders in this field. A general view of Jewish contributions is given in

BIOLOGY, JEWS IN 2:362-67

The following are the most important Jewish biologists and biochemists, in chronological order:

Bloch, Marcus Eliezer 2:401 (G)
Cohn, Ferdinand Julius 3:259 (G)
Sachs, Julius 9:304 (G)
Strasburger, Eduard 10:73 (G)
Ascherson, Paul 1:535 (G)
Auerbach, Leopold 1:612 (G)
Remak, Robert 9:131 (G)
Errera, Leo Abraham 4:156 (Be)
Metchnikoff, Élie 7:508 (Ru, F)
Aharoni, Israel 1:137 (P)
Loeb, Jacques 7:154-55 (G, US)
Taubenhaus, Jacob J. (10:177-78 (US)
Lipman, Jacob Goodale 7:73-74 (US)
Ezekiel, Walter Naphtali 4:225 (US)
Waksman, Selman A. 10:442 (US)
Rosen, Joseph A. 9:202-3 (US)
Pincus, Gregory 8:533-34 (US)
Muller, Hermann Joseph 8:34 (US, Ru, Sc)
Friedmann, Herbert 4:457 (US)
Funk, Casimir 4:481 (F, G, E, US)
Fasten, Nathan 4:249 (US)
Goldforb, Abraham Jules 5:22 (US)
Goldschmidt, Richard Benedikt 5:31-32 (G, Japan, US)
Hyman, Libbie Henrietta 5:515 (US)
Aaronsohn, Aaron 1:8-9 (P)
Warburg, Otto Heinrich 10:459-60 (G)
Neuberg, Carl 8:155 (G, P, US)
Alsberg, Carl Lucas (d. 1940) 1:209 (US)

OUTLINE 82: JEWS IN CHEMISTRY

The origins of chemistry go back into the pseudo-science of alchemy, which was the first to attempt to discover the elements which compose all substances. The part that Jews played in this primitive science is described in

ALCHEMY 1:164-66

A special article is devoted to
Maria Hebrea 7:356

Jews have participated in all fields of modern chemistry. This is recapitulated in

CHEMISTRY 3:125-31

The following are the most important Jewish chemists, arranged according to countries:

Austria

Lieben, Adolf 7:49-50
Goldschmidt, Guido 5:28
Lippmann, Eduard 7:75
Lippmann, Edmund Oskar von 7:74-75

Belgium

Errera, Jacques 4:156

England

Mond, Ludwig 7:618
Mond, Sir Robert Ludwig 7:618
Meldola, Raphael 7:455
Cohen, Julius Berend 3:248
Weizmann, Chaim 10:495-99
Copisarow, Maurice 3:365
Heilbron, Ian Morris 5:294
Levinstein, Ivan 6:636
Fodor, Andor 4:346-47

Germany

Meyer, Victor 7:518-19
Caro, Heinrich 3:49
Magnus, Heinrich Gustav 7:278
Liebermann, Carl 7:52
Meyer, Lothar Julius 7:516
Lunge, Georg 7:237
Goldschmidt, Hans 5:28-29
Wallach, Otto 10:446-47
Frank, Adolf 4:389
Haber, Fritz 5:143
Liebreich, Oskar Mathias Eugen 7:56
Willstätter, Richard 10:524-25
Caro, Nikodem 3:51
Bechhold, Heinrich 2:127
Marckwald, Willy 7:346

Holland

Cohen, Ernst Julius 3:241

Russia

Karpov, Lev Iakolevich 6:326

United States

Loeb, Morris 7:157
Woolf, Albert Edward 10:571
Mendel, Lafayette Benedict 7:468
Gomberg, Moses 5:49
Levene, Phoebus A. 6:618-19
Fajans, Kasimir 4:234
Stieglitz, Julius O. 10:65
Arnstein, Henry 1:486
Kharasch, Morris Selig 6:374

OUTLINE 83: JEWS IN CHESS

Chess has been a favorite game of Jews ever since it first became known to them in the Middle Ages. It was given a place of honor distinguishing it from other games, and an unusually large number of Jews became noted chessmasters. The general article on the subject is

CHESS 3:133-34

There are articles on the following important Jewish players, arranged chronologically:
Horwitz, Bernard 5:461 (E)

Zukertort, Johannes Hermann 10:676 (G, E)
Gunsberg, Isidor 5:130 (E)
Judd, Max 6:251 (US)
Steinitz, William 10:48 (A, E, US)
Lasker, Emanuel 6:539 (G, US)
Janowski, David 6:38 (F)
Kupchik, Abraham 6:489-90 (US)
Mieses, Jacques 7:543 (G)
Nimzowitsch, Aron 8:222 (Latvia)
Reti, Richard 9:144 (Cz)
Tarrasch, Siegbert 10:176 (G)
Tartakower, Sevelij 10:176 (Ru)
Reshevsky, Samuel 9:136-37 (US)
Botwinnik, Misha 2:485 (Ru)
Flohr, Salo 4:330 (Latvia)
Horowitz, Israel A. 5:459 (US)
Kashdan, Isaac I. 6:326-27 (US)
Fine, Reuben 4:304 (US)
Reinfeld, Fred 9:119-20 (US)
Karff, N. May 6:320 (US)

OUTLINE 84: JEWS IN DENTISTRY

Artificial teeth are mentioned in the Talmud, proving that at that time Jews had some knowledge of dentistry. It was in the modern period, however, that individual Jews began to make contributions to dental science as technicians and teachers.

The general article on the subject is

DENTISTRY, JEWS IN 3:536-37

There are individual articles on the following dentists, arranged chronologically:
Hart, John Isaac 5:228 (US)
Greenbaum, Leo 5:95 (US)
Weinstein, Louis J. 10:491 (US)
Chayes, Herman E. S. 3:124 (US)
Hellman, Milo 5:312 (US)
Kronfeld, Rudolf 6:477 (A, US)
Gottlieb, Bernhard 5:71-72 (A, P, US)
Weinberger, Bernhard Wolf 10:488 (US)
Schroff, Joseph 9:426-27 (US)
Bear, Harry 2:123 (US)
Diamond, Moses 3:560 (US)
Schour, Isaac 9:425 (US)

OUTLINE 85: JEWS AS EDUCATORS

While the Jews always had an elaborate educational system of their own, it was not until modern times that they were permitted to participate in secular education. The first Jewish educators were the creators of private schools; subsequently a large number taught in universities and, finally, in the public schools. In the United States, in particular, many Jews have become administrative officers in the public school system.

The part played by Jews in universities is given in

UNIVERSITIES 10:363-76

The following are the most important Jewish educators, arranged in chronological order:
Mordecai, Jacob 7:644 (US)
Wertheimer, Joseph Ritter von 10:505 (A)
Epstein, Ephraim M. 4:141-42 (US)
Bamberger, Gabriel 2:58 (G, US)
Salomon, Otto Aron 9:325 (Sw)
Kármán, Mór 6:324-25 (Hu)
Slomann, Emil 9:568 (D)
Sachs, Julius 9:304 (US)
Richman, Julia 9:158-59 (US)
Leipziger, Henry Marcus 6:602 (US)
Trier, Herman Martin 10:307 (D)
Adler, Felix 1:91-92 (US)
Loewenberg, Jakob 7:163-64 (G)
Stroock, Moses J. 10:86 (US)
Veit, Benjamin 10:399 (US)
Mankiewicz, Frank 7:324 (US)
Teixeira, Anisio Spinola 10:188 (Brazil)
Flexner, Abraham 4:326-28 (US)
Gans, Bird Stein 4:510-11 (US)
Gruenberg, Benjamin Charles 5:108 (US)
Nusbaum, Louis 8:258 (US)
Abelson, Paul 1:20-21 (US)
Goldwasser, Israel Edwin 5:41 (US)
Deutsch, Monroe E. 3:555 (US)
Kandel, Isaac Leon 6:304 (E, US)
Bamberger, Florence Eilau 2:58 (US)
Scott, Miriam Finn 9:447 (US)
Bildersee, Adele 2:352 (US)
Lieberman, Elias 7:51 (US)
Cohen, I. David 3:245-46 (US)
Cohen, (A.) Broderick 3:239-40 (US)
Klapper, Paul 6:409-10 (US)
Reh, Frank 9:113 (US)
Schoen, Max 9:416 (US)
Cohen, Joseph George 3:247 (US)
Hart, Ivor B. 5:227-28 (E)
Naumburg, Margaret 8:133 (US)
Gottschall, Morton 5:74 (US)
Meister, Morris 7:448 (US)
Marshall, James 7:379-80 (US)
Silverman, Herbert A. 9:538 (E)
Simon, Henry W. 9:546 (US)

OUTLINE 86: JEWS IN FINANCE

The participation of the Jews in finance resulted in an unusual and unexpected way. There were Jewish traders as early as in Bible times, but Jews were never bankers or money-lenders until well into the Middle Ages. It was only when their position became insecure from attacks that they were forced to seek an occupation which did not depend on owning real estate or on permanent location; and since the church law forbade the taking of interest on loans by Christians from Christians, the Jews were almost compelled to take up money lending to secure their livelihood and ensure their welcome. At the beginning of modern times some Jews acted as fiscal agents for princes. With the coming of the mercantile age, Jewish money lenders and agents suddenly found themselves in the forefront of the new commercial expansion, and they retained their position, chiefly as private bankers, through the development that accompanied the industrial revolution. They have participated to a far less extent in the public banking of modern times.

The comprehensive article on the subject is

FINANCE, JEWS IN 4:289-302

For the beginnings of Jewish financial activity in the Middle Ages and early modern times, see Loans 7:149-50

MONEY LENDING 7:618-22

Exchange, Bills of 4:204
Court Jews 3:384-85

The following were early Jewish money lenders:
Aaron of Lincoln 1:6 (E)
Aaron of York 1:6-7 (E)
Szerencsés, Imre 10:144-45 (Hu)

The following are the more important Jewish financiers, arranged according to countries and chronologically:

Various Countries in Europe

Rothschild 9:235-46

England

Hambro, Joseph 5:192
Gideon, Sampson 4:607-8
Schuster 9:431-32
Stern, David 10:53
Swaythling, First Baron 10:111-12
Speyer, Edgar 9:694
Sassoon 9:373-79
Seligman, Isaac N. 9:468

France

Bischoffsheim 2:383
Hirsch, Baron Maurice de 5:375-77
Fould, Achille 4:360-61
Péreire, Isaac 8:435
Péreire, Emile 8:435

Germany and Austria

Speyer, Georg 9:694
Mendelssohn, Joseph 7:471
Salomonsohn 9:326-27
Bleichroeder, Gerson 2:391
Warburg 10:453, 458
Goldschmidt-Rothschild 5:33
Oppenheim, Salomon, Jr. 8:307-8
Wassermann, Oskar 10:474
Goldschmidt, Jakob 5:29-30
Arnstein, von 1:485
Eskeles, Bernhard 4:165
Itzig, Daniel 5:640-41
Ephraim, Veitel Heine 4:135-36

Seeligmann von Eichthal 9:458
Königswarter 6:447
Melchior, Carl 7:453-54
Ladenburg 6:507

Russia

Stiglitz 10:65
Günzburg 5:130-32
Poliakoff, Jacob 8:579
Poliakoff, Lazar 8:579-80

Poland

Wawelberg, Hipolit 10:478

Roumania

Blank, Maurichev 2:388

Hungary

Ullmann, Adolf (de Baranyavár) 10:340
Kohner, Adolf 6:435
Lánczy, Leó 6:521
Kornfeld, Zsigmond 6:456-57
Wahrmann, Mor 10:441
Madarassy-Beck 7:267-68
Székely, Ferenc 10:142
Hatvany-Deutsch 5:249-50
Krausz, Simon 6:468

United States

Salomon, Haym 9:322-24
Guggenheim 5:116-23
Speyer, James 9:698-99
Seligman, Joseph 9:468-69
Seligman, Jesse 9:468
Loeb, Solomon 7:157
Loeb, James 7:155-56
Schiff, Jacob H. 9:400-3
Warburg, Felix 10:454-58
Schiff, Mortimer L. 9:403-4
Lehman, Mayer 6:596
Lehman, Arthur 6:592
Meyer, Eugene, Jr. 7:515-16

OUTLINE 87: JEWS IN INDUSTRY

The history of Jews in industry is closely connected with their rise in finance. With the development of commerce and manufacture from the latter part of the 18th century on, Jews participated in increasing numbers in the developing industries, first of Europe and later of America. To this they brought their skill in trading and the experience of Jewish artisans. As a rule, their work was pioneering; they did not enter old established industries, but developed new fields.

The following articles deal with certain special fields of industry:

Dye Industry, Jews in 3:615-16
Diamond Trade, Jews in 3:558-59
Needle Trades 8:141-44

Jewish industrialists who receive articles are

Seeligman von Eichthal 9:458 (G)
Lämel, Simon Edler von 6:513 (A)
Hirsch, Aron 5:373 (G)
Rée, Hartvig Philip 9:100 (D)
Löwy, Izsák 7:221 (Hu)
Kohner 6:435 (Hu)
Reichenheim, Leonor 9:115 (G)
Löbel, Jacob 7:150-51 (Ro)
Behrens, Jacob 2:137-38 (E)
Sassoon 9:373-79 (India, China)
Kohn, Tobias 6:434-35 (A, US)
Loewe, Ludwig 7:162-63 (G)
Samuelson, Sir Bernard 9:352-53 (E)
Poliakoff, Samuel S. 8:580 (Ru)
Salamon, Nahum 9:318 (E)
Schey von Koromla 9:398 (Hu, A)
Becker, Moritz 2:129 (G)
Levinstein, Ivan 6:636 (E)
Montefiore, Georges Levi 7:629-30 (Be)
Petschek 8:472 (Cz)
Guggenheim 5:116-23 (US)
Van den Bergh 10:392 (Ho, E)
Morris, Nelson 7:656 (US)
Mond, Ludwig 7:618 (E)
Ballin, Albert 2:50-51 (G)
Rathenau, Emil 9:81 (G)
Poliakoff, Lazar 8:579-80 (Ru)
Deutsch de la Meurthe, Henry 3:556 (F)
Deutsch de la Meurthe, Émile 3:556-56 (F)
Marks, Samuel 7:362 (S Af)
Arnhold, Eduard 1:484 (G)
Baron, Bernhard 2:89 (US, E)
Netter, Carl Leopold 8:153 (G)
Deutsch, Felix 3:553 (G)
Cone 3:325-26 (US)
Weiller, Lazare 10:487-88 (F)
Bernheim, Isaac Wolfe 2:229-30 (US)
Albu, Sir George 1:163 (S Af)
Rosenthal, Philipp 9:222 (G)
Melchett, Lord Alfred 7:451-52 (E)
Kaszab, Aladar 6:334 (Hu)
Joel, Solomon Barnato 6:161-62 (S Af)
Littauer, Lucius Nathan 7:138 (US)
Mamroth, Paul 7:308 (G)
Citroen, André Gustave 3:217 (F)
Mond, Sir Robert Ludwig 7:618 (E)
Mond, Emil 7:617 (E)
Caro, Nikodem 3:51 (G)
Richardson, Sir Lewis 9:157 (S Af)
Blum, Albert 2:415-16 (US)
Bloch, Sir Maurice 2:402 (Sc)
Brown, David Abraham 2:561-62 (US)
Rutenberg, Pinchas 9:286 (Ru, P)
Waldes, Heinrich 10:444 (Cz)
Silverberg, Paul 9:537 (G)
Zagajski, Mieczyslaus 10:625 (Po)
Kon, Oskar 6:445 (Po)
Strelsin, Alfred A. 10:84-85 (US)
Dreyfuss, Henry 3:600 (US)

OUTLINE 88: JEWS AS INVENTORS

Despite the fact that most Jews have followed occupations that give little or no scope for invention, there has been a respectable number of Jewish inventors in the course of history. A list of these is given in

SCIENCE AND INVENTION 9:443-44

The following articles, arranged in chronological order, deal with Jewish inventors in numerous fields:

Maria Hebra 7:356
Colorni, Abramo 3:305-6 (I)
Isaacs, Jacob 5:598 (US)
Stern, Abraham Jacob 10:51 (Po)
Gompertz, Lewis 5:54 (E)
Samuda, Jacob 9:345 (E)
Jacobi, Moritz Hermann 6:16 (Ru)
Valobra, Sansone 10:390 (I)
Reis, Philipp 9:121 (G)
Slonimsky, Hayim Selig 9:569 (Po)
Marcus, Siegfried 7:350 (G, A)
Becker, Moritz 2:129 (G)
Schwarz, David 9:435 (A, Ru)
Zalinski, Edmund Louis Gray 10:626-27 (US)
Aron, Hermann 1:486-87 (G)
Popper, Joseph 8:600-1 (A)
Levy, Louis Edward 7:13 (US)
Kitsee, Isador 6:408 (US)
Ayrton, Hertha 1:651 (E)
Berliner, Emile 2:219-21 (US)
Abraham, Rudolf 1:46-47 (G)
Goldschmidt, Hans 5:28-29 (G)
Hubert, Conrad 5:477 (US)
Ries, Elias Elkan 9:161 (US)
Lieben, Robert von 7:50 (A)
Artom, Alessandro 1:515 (I)
Levy, Max 7:14-15 (US)
Belais, David 2:144-45 (US)
Marks, Louis Benedict 7:361 (US)
Goldschmidt, Rudolf 5:32 (G)
Silverman, Alexander 9:537 (US)
Dubilier, William 3:604 (US)
Naumburg, Robert Elkan 8:133-34 (US)

OUTLINE 89: JEWS IN JOURNALISM

Jews began to participate in modern journalism about the middle of the 19th century, and since that time there have been a respectable number of Jewish writers, editors and publishers in many countries of Europe and in the United States. An especially noteworthy Jewish contribution has been the creation of news-gathering agencies, in which field they were pioneers. Jewish journalists have varied considerably in their political and social views, as expressed in the current periodicals. In addition, there have been a number of Jewish journalists who have created a separate press for their fellow Jews.

The comprehensive article on the subject is

PERIODICALS AND PRESS 8:437-57

The most important Jewish journalists in the public press, arranged by countries and in chronological order, are

Austria

Kuranda, Ignaz 6:491
Benedikt, Moritz 2:170-71
Herzl, Theodor 5:337-38

Denmark

Brandes, Carl Edward 2:500

England

Reuter, Paul Julius 9:145
Levy, Joseph Moses 7:13
Blumenfeld, Ralph David 2:419-20
Wolf, Lucien 10:553-54
Magnus, Laurie 7:278-79
Southwood, Baron 9:669

France

Blowitz, Henri 2:415

Germany

Börne, Karl Ludwig 2:474-476
Heine, Heinrich 5:297-301
Wolf, Bernhard 10:557
Mosse, Rudolf 8:20
Ullstein, Leopold 10:340-42
Stein, August 10:37-38
Beer, Max 2:133-34
Nathan, Paul 8:110
Harden, Maximilian 5:214
Wolff, Theodor 10:557-58
Bernhard, Georg 2:228
Schwarzschild, Leopold 9:438
Kerr, Alfred 6:365-66

Holland

Vaz Dias 10:396-97

Hungary

Falk, Miksa 4:238
Vészi, József 10:410-11
Hevesi, Lajos 5:349
Kunfi, Zsigmond 6:488

Japan

Fleischer, Benjamin W. 4:324-25

United States

Noah, Mordecai Manuel 8:226-27
De Young, Michael 3:501
Pulitzer, Joseph 9:34-35
Rosewater 9:226-27
Ochs, Adolph S. 8:280-81
De Casseres, Benjamin 3:494-95
Koenigsberg, Moses 6:425-26
Franklin, Fabian 4:414

Bernstein, Herman 2:235-36
Adler, Emanuel P. 1:90-91
Marcosson, Isaac F. 7:346-47
Strunsky, Simeon 10:87-88
Tobenkin, Elias 10:258
Stern, J. David 10:57
Block, Paul (d. 1941) 2:404
Seldes, George 9:463-64
Haldeman-Julius, Emanuel 5:177-78
Swope, Herbert Bayard 10:116
Lawrence, David 6:564
Adams, Franklin P. 1:80
Levine, Isaac Don 6:633
Lippmann, Walter 7:75-77
Adler, Julius Ochs 1:95
Sulzberger, Arthur Hays 10:98
Winchell, Walter 10:527-28
Grafton, Samuel 5:81-82
Mayer, Eugene, Jr. 7:515-16
Backer, George 2:23
Backer, Dorothy S. 9:404

The following articles deal with periodicals created for Jewish readers; they are arranged in the order of their founding:

Allgemeine Zeitung des Judentums 1:188 (G)
Jewish Chronicle 6:95-96 (E)
American Israelite 1:241-42 (US)
American Hebrew 1:238-41 (US)
National Jewish Monthly 8:123 (US)
Jewish Quarterly Review 6:140 (E, US)
Haint 5:172 (Po)
Hadoar 5:150-51 (US)
Dawar 3:492 (P)

The following are the chief contributors to and editors of Jewish periodicals, arranged in chronological order and by languages:

Anglo-Jewish

Leeser, Isaac 6:588 (US)
Wise, Isaac Mayer 10:539-41 (US)
Wise, Leo 10:542 (US)
Cowen, Philip 3:391 (d. 1943) (US)
Mosessohn, Nehemiah 8:16 (US)
Greenberg, Leopold J. 5:97 (E)
Landau, Jacob 6:524 (Ho, E, US)
Landman, Isaac 6:527-29 (US)
Rittenberg, Louis 9:169 (US)
Wise, James Waterman 10:541 (US)

Hebrew and Yiddish

Braudes, Reuben Asher 2:506 (Po, A)
Bader, Gershom 2:24-25 (Po, US)
Goldberg, Abraham (d. 1942) 5:12-13 (US)

Hebrew

Brill, Jehiel 2:529-30 (P, F, G, E)
Smolenskin, Peretz 9:573-74 (R, A)
Sokolow, Nahum 9:590-92 (Po, G, E)
Frischman, David 4:462-63 (Ru)
Brainin, Reuben 2:493 (Ru, A, G, US)
Brenner, Joseph Hayim 2:518-19 (Ru, P)
Feuerstein, Abigdor 4:284-85 (P)

Yiddish

Cahan, Abraham 2:624 (US)
Litwakov, Moses 7:145 (Ru)
Olgin, Moissaye J. 8:295 (Ru, US)
Revusky, Abraham 9:150 (Ru, US, P)
Kantorovitch, Chaim 6:309-10 (US)

The following organization was created for the collection and dissemination of Jewish news:

Jewish Telegraphic Agency 6:142-43

OUTLINE 90: JEWS IN LITERATURE

It is but natural that the part played by Jews in modern literature should loom large. The Jews were always a literary people—for centuries literature was the only way in which they could express their creative talents. When the opportunity came to enter the world of modern life, they turned from writing for Jews and in specifically Jewish languages to writing for the general public in all modern languages. They have contributed far more than a proportionate number of novelists, poets, dramatists, essayists and journalists.

A general view of the Jewish contribution to world literature is given in the articles

LITERATURE ON AND BY JEWS 7:100-25

AMERICAN LITERATRE ON AND BY JEWS 1:262-70

The following are the most important Jewish writers, divided according to languages and chronologically:

English

a. In the British Empire

Florio, John 4:345
Disraeli, Benjamin 3:570-73
Aguilar, Grace 1:131-32
Farjeon 4:248
Zangwill, Israel 10:627-29
Gordon, Samuel 5:65-66
Wolfe, Humbert 10:555-56
Guedalla, Philip 5:116
Golding, Louis 5:22-23
Sassoon, Siegfried 9:376-77
Stern, Gladys B. 10:54-55
Tobias, Lily 10:259
Merrick, Leonard 7:495-96

b. In the United States

Judah, Samuel B. H. 6:232
Harby, Isaac 5:213
Noah, Mordecai Manuel 8:226-27
Moise, Penina 7:612-13
Cahan, Abraham 2:624
Hurst, Fanny 5:505-6
Yezierska, Anzia 10:597-98
Ferber, Edna 4:276-77
Brudno, Ezra 2:565
Glass, Montague 4:618
Oppenheim, James 8:306

Tobenkin, Elias 10:258
Nyburg, Sidney 8:260
Cournos, John 3:384
Lewisohn, Ludwig 7:26
Stein, Gertrude 10:38
Gold, Michael 5:11-12
Hecht, Ben 5:288
Fineman, Irving 4:304
Halper, Albert 5:185
Frank, Waldo 4:396-97
Brinig, Myron 2:531
Weidman, Jerome 10:483
Samuel, Maurice 9:351
Seaver, Edwin 9:452
Zugsmith, Leane 10:676
Cohen, Octavus Roy 3:254-55
Bercovici, Konrad 2:191-92
Nathan, Robert 8:110-11
Cohen, Lester 3:249-50
Crane, Nathalia 3:395
Komroff, Manuel 6:444-45
Maltz, Albert 7:307
Stone, Irving 10:69-70
Untermeyer, Louis 10:378
Lieberman, Elias 7:51
Belasco, David 2:145-47
Klein, Charles 6:413-14
Kaufman, George S. 6:341-42
Behrman, Samuel Nathaniel 2:138
Odets, Clifford 8:283-84
Rice, Elmer 9:156
Lazarus, Emma 6:568-69
Rukeyser, Muriel 9:275-76
Deutsch, Babette 3:552-53
Parker, Dorothy 8:402

German

Süsskind von Trimberg 10:108-9
Akerman, Rachel 1:144
Kuh, Ephraim Moses 6:484-85
Robert, Ludwig 9:175
Beer, Michael 2:134
Saphir, Moritz Gottlieb 9:365-66
Heine, Henrich 5:297-301
Börne, Karl Ludwig 2:474-76
Auerbach, Berthold 1:611-12
Rodenburg, Julius 9:180
Ebers, Georg 3:619
Lewald, Fanny 7:19-20
Glück, Barbara Elizabeth 4:624
Landesmann, Heinrich 6:527
Kalisch, David 6:294
L'Arronge, Adolf 6:536
Bernstein, Aaron 2:232-33
Kompert, Leopold 6:444
Franzos, Karl Emil 4:419
Hirschfeld, Georg 5:381
Fulda, Ludwig 4:470
Schnitzler, Arthur 9:413-15
Beer-Hofmann, Richard 2:135-36
Wassermann, Jakob 10:472-74
Engländer, Richard 4:131
Friedell, Egon 4:447
Zweig, Stefan 10:680
Salten, Felix 9:330
Kalfa, Franz 6:277-78
Wolfskehl, Karl 10:560
Gundolf, Friedrich 5:130

Ludwig, Emil 7:230-32
Lissauer, Ernst 7:84
Mombert, Alfred 7:616
Werfel, Franz 10:501-2
Brod, Max 2:537-38
Frank, Bruno 4:389
Feuchtwanger, Lion 4:283-84
Neumann, Robert 8:160-61
Zweig, Arnold 10:679-80
Neumann, Alfred 8:157
Döblin, Alfred 3:581
Baum, Vicki 2:115-16
Katz, Herz Wolff 6:336

French

Halévy, Ludovic 5:179-80
Manuel, Eugène 7:335-36
Mendès, Catulle 7:477-78
Kahn, Gustave 6:287-88
Proust, Marcel 9:5-6
Savoir, Alfred de 9:385
Croisset, François de 3:423
Nozière, Fernand 8:247-48
Crémieux, Hector Jonathan 3:406-7
Sée, Edmond 9:457
Valabrègue, Albin 10:389
Valabrègue, Antoine 10:389
Bernstein, Henry 2:235
Bernard, Tristan 2:225
Suarès, André 10:92
Maurois, André 7:415
Bloch, Jean Richard 2:400
Spire, André 10:9-10
Franck, Henri 4:386
Fleg, Edmond 4:322-23

Hungarian

Kiss, József 6:406-7
Ágai, Adolf 1:111
Kóbor, Tamás 6:423
Biró, Lajos 2:372
Heltai, Jenö 5:313
Molnár, Ferenc 7:614-15
Karinthy, Frigyes 6:321

Szep, Ernö 10:143-44
Ignotus, Hugó 5:537-38
Foldi, Mihaly 4:347-48
Erdös, Renée 4:150-51
Makai, Emil 7:298-99
Kiss, Arnold 6:406
Patai, József 8:411-12
Zsolt, Béla 10:674-75

Italian

Fiorentino, Salamone 4:310
Revere, Giuseppe 9:149
Lopez, Sabatino 7:191-92

Svevo, Italo, 10:111
Orvieto, Angelo 8:331
Segre, Dino 9:461
Vivanti, Annie 10:429

Scandinavian Languages

Hertz, Henrik 5:332-33
Goldschmidt, Meir Aaron 5:31
Nathansen, Henri 8:112
Brandes, Georg 2:500-2
Levertin, Oscar 6:620
Elkan, Sophie 4:83

Dutch

Costa, Isaac da 3:374
Heijermans, Hermann 5:293-94
Querido, Israel 9:46
Haan, Jacob Israel de 5:139
Van Praag, Siegfried Emanuel 10:393-94

Spanish

Rojas, Fernando de 9:183-84
Glusberg, Samuel 4:628
Gerchunoff, Alberto 4:539
Grunberg, Carlos Moises 5:111

Polish

Klaczko, Juliusz 6:409
Tuwim, Julian 10:329-30
Wittlin, Józef 10:550
Arnsztajn, Felicya 1:486

Russian

Frug, Simon Samuel 4:466-67
Ehrenburg, Ilya 4:17
Wengeroff 10:501
Babel, Isaac Emanuilovich 2:8-9

Roumanian

Ronetti-Roman 9:194
Celibi, Moise 3:73
Ludo, J. 7:230

OUTLINE 91: JEWS IN MATHEMATICS

Jews were interested in mathematics as far back as ancient times, since certain mathematical calculations were required by the ritual law. For the most part, however, they were content to follow the discoveries of the Greeks. In the Middle Ages a few Jews were mathematicians, and only in modern times did they begin to make numerous contributions to mathematical knowledge.

The general article on the subject is

MATHEMATICS, JEWS IN 7:408-11

Among the Jewish mathematicians of the Middle Ages were

Abraham bar Hiyya 1:40-41 (S)
Gersonides 4:592-93 (F)
Delmedigo, Joseph 3:518-19 (Gr, I, G, A)
Motot, Simeon 8:23

The most noted Jewish mathematicians of modern times are

Jacobi, Carl Gustav 6:15 (G)
Cantor, Georg 3:18-19 (G)
Sylvester, James Joseph 10:118 (E)
Einstein, Albert 4:29-33 (G, Swi, US)

Other articles on Jewish mathematicians, in alphabetical order, are

Ascoli, Giulio 1:535 (I)
Baer, Asher 2:29 (Ru, P)

Beke, Manó 2:143 (Hu)
Bernstein, Benjamin Abraham 2:234 (US)
Besso, Davide 2:249 (I)
Blaschke, Wilhelm 2:388-89 (A, G)
Bogyó, Samu 2:439 (Hu)
Brodetsky, Selig 2:539 (E)
Cantor, Moritz 3:19 (G)
Cohen, Abraham 3:236-37 (US)
Dantzig, Tobias 3:468 (US)
Dikstein, Samuel 3:565 (Po)
Dresden, Arnold 3:596 (US)
Eisenstein, Ferdinand Max 4:39 (G)
Emanuel, David 4:95 (Ro)
Fekete, Michael 4:269-70 (Hu, P)
Filipowski, Zebi Hirsch 4:289 (E)
Fraenkel, Abraham Halevi 4:365 (G)
Fuchs, Immanuel Lazarus 4:468 (G)
Ginsburg, Jekuthiel 4:612 (US)
Gompertz, Benjamin 5:52 (E)
Hadamard, Jacques 5:146 (F)
Halphen, Georges Henri 5:187 (F)
Kasner, Edward 6:331 (US)
Koenigsberger, Leo 6:426 (G)
Kronecker, Leopold 6:477 (G)
Landau, Edmund George Hermann 6:522
 (G, P)
Lefschetz, Solomon 6:589 (US)
Levi, Beppo 6:622-23 (I)
Levi-Civita, Tullio 6:627 (I)
Lévy, Lucien 7:13-14 (F)
Levy, Paul 7:16 (F)
Lichtenstein, Leon 7:48 (G)
Lipschitz, Rudolf Otto Sigismund 7:78 (G)
Loewy, Alfred 7:166 (G)
Loria, Gino 7:193-94 (I)
Milhaud, Gaston Samuel 7:560-61 (F)
Minkowski, Hermann 7:569 (G, Swi)
Mises, Richard Martin, Edler von 7:580
 (G, T, US)
Mordell, Louis Joel 7:644 (US)
Ostrowski, Alexander 8:334 (G, Swi)
Padoa, Allessandro 8:342 (I)
Pasch, Moritz 8:406 (G)
Pringsheim, Alfred 8:645 (G)
Réthi, Mór 9:144 (Hu)
Ritt, Joseph Fels 9:168 (US)
Rosanes, Jacob 9:200 (G)
Rosenbach, Joseph B. 9:205 (US)
Schapira, Hermann 9:389-90 (G)
Schlesinger, Ludwig 9:409 (G, Hu)
Schur, Issai 9:430-31 (G, P)
Schwarzschild, Karl 9:437-38 (G)
Steinhaus, Hugo Dyonise 10:47 (Po)
Stone, Charles Arthur 10:69 (US)
Szegö, Gabriel 10:141-42 (G, US)
Wiener, Norbert 10:515 (US)
Zariski, Oscar 10:630 (US)

Of special mathematical interest are the articles

Euclid 4:191
Finkelstein, Salo 4:307-8 (Po, US)

OUTLINE 92: JEWS IN MEDICINE

Jews have always played a large part in medical science. In ancient times the hygienic regulations of the Law made it important for rabbis to acquire medical knowledge. In the Middle Ages Jewish physicians were famous. In modern times there are hundreds of Jews who have made contributions in all fields of medical research and practice.

The general articles on the subject are

MEDICINE 7:434-36
HYGIENE OF THE JEWS 5:509-14
PHYSICIANS 8:523-27

The chief early physicians whose teachings were followed by Jews were

Hippocrates 5:370-71   Galen 4:492

The following are among the most important Jewish physicians prior to the middle of the 17th century, arranged in chronological order:

Asaph Judaeus 1:530-31
Masarjawiah 7:393 (Mesopotamia)
Tabari, Sahl al 10:152 (Asia)
Donnolo, Sabbatai 3:590 (I)
Hasdai ibn Shaprut 5:236 (S)
Maimonides § 4. 7:294-96 (Morocco, Egypt)
Nathanael 8:112 (Egypt)
Faraj ben Salim 4:246 (I)
Mantino, Jacob 7:334 (I)
Zarfati, Samuel 10:630 (F, I)
Sarah 9:367 (G)
Zerlina 10:640 (G)
Bernal, Maestro 2:223 (S)
Amatus Lusitanus 1:222 (S, I, T)
Loans, Jacob ben Jehiel 7:150 (G)
Lopez, Rodrigo 7:189-91 (Pt, E)
Pomis, David de 8:585 (I)
Zacutus Lusitanus 10:623 (Pt, Ho)
Castro, Balthasar Orobio 3:61-62 (S, F, Ho)
Bueno 2:579-80 (Ho)
Troki, Abraham ben Josiah 10:311 (Ru)
Zahalon, Jacob ben Isaac 10:626 (I)

Pioneer Jewish physicians in modern Europe, arranged in chronological order, were

Garcia da Orta 4:514 (Pt, India)
Cohen, Tobias 3:256 (Po, T)
Mendes, Moses 7:480 (Pt, E)
Schomberg, Meyer Löw 9:418 (G, E)
Schomberg, Raphael 9:418 (E)
Sanchez, Antonio Nunes 9:358-59
 (Pt, Ho, Hu, F)
Marcus, Moses 7:349 (Hu, G)
Abraham, Mayer 1:46 (G)
Fonseca, Daniel de 4:355-56 (Pt, F, T, Ro)
Bernhard, Abraham 2:227 (Ru)
Koreff, David Ferdinand 6:454 (G, F, A)
Bégin, Louis Jacques 2:136 (F)
Kosch, Raphael 6:458-59 (G)
Romberg, Moritz Heinrich 9:186-87 (G)

Pereira, Jonathan 8:434-35 (E)
Drey, Dr. 3:596 (Ro)
Henle, Friedrich Gustav Jacob 5:314-15 (G)
Melchior, Nathan Gerson 7:452-53 (D)
Lumbroso, Baron Abram 7:234-35 (Tunisia)

Early Jewish physicians in America, in chronological order, were

Lumbrozo, Jacob (John) 7:235
Siccary 9:525
Abrahams, Isaac 1:47
Sheftall, Moses 9:500
Hart, Joel 5:228
Motta, Jacob de la 8:23
De Leon, Abraham 3:498
Horwitz, (Jonas and) Jonathan Phineas 5:461
Cohen, Joshua I. 3:234-36
De Leon, David Camden 3:499
Pollak, Simon 8:582
Liebermann, Charles H. 7:52-53
Bensadon, Joseph 2:186
Waterman, Sigismond 10:476
Mayer, Nathan 7:425
Solis-Cohen, Jacob da Silva 9:634

Famous Jewish physicians of modern times, in chronological order, are

Traube, Ludwig, pathologist 10:296 (G)
Cohnheim, Julius, pathologist 3:261-62 (G)
Baruch, Simon, surgeon and hygienist 2:99-100 (US)
Neisser, Albert, dermatologist 8:149 (G)
Steinach, Eugen, physiologist 10:40-41 (A)
Haffkine, Waldemar Mordecai, bacteriologist 5:151-52 (Ru, Swi, F, India)
Wassermann, August von, immunologist 10:471-72 (G)
Rosenau, Milton Joseph, sanitarian 9:204 (US)
Flexner, Simon, bacteriologist 4:328-29 (US)
Landsteiner, Karl, physiologist 6:531 (A, Ho, US)
Goldberger, Joseph, pathologist 5:16-17 (US)
Voronoff, Serge, surgeon 10:433-34 (Ru, F, US)
Besredka, Alexandre, immunologist 2:244 (F)
Schick, Béla, pediatrician 9:398-99 (Hu, A, US)
Buerger, Leo, surgeon 2:582-83 (US)
Bárány, Robert, anatomist 2:79 (A, Sw)
Stern (Shtern), Lina Solomonovna, physiologist 10:57-58 (Ru, Swi)
Warburg, Otto H., pathologist 10:459-60 (G)
Meyerhof, Otto, physiologist 7:521-22 (G, US)
Berman, Louis, endocrinologist 2:221 (US)
Kahn, Reuben Leon, bacteriologist 6:290-91 (US)
Zondek, Bernard, gynecologist 10:672-73 (G, Sw, P)
Sakel, Manfred, psychiatrist 9:317 (A, G, US)
Brodie, Maurice, bacteriologist 2:540 (C, US)

There is a noteworthy group of Jewish psycho-analysts

Freud, Sigmund 4:441-43 (A)

Adler, Alfred 1:87-88 (A, US)
Stekel, Wilhelm 10:51 (A, E)
Rank, Otto 9:70 (A, F, US)
Reik, Theodor 9:116-17 (A, G, US)
Brill, Abraham Arden 2:529 (US)
Coriat, Isidor Henry 3:369 (US)
An article is devoted to the medical martyr
Reinhart, Alfred Seymour 9:120-21 (US)

OUTLINE 93: JEWS IN MUSIC

It is generally recognized that Jews have played a tremendous part in the development of music in modern times. The list of Jewish composers, singers, instrumentalists and musicologists is extremely long and varied. It can be fairly said that had it not been for Jewish musicians and students and patrons of music, the progress and the appreciation of music would have been much inferior to those of the present time.

For music created by the Jews for themselves, see the outline on JEWISH MUSIC. The earliest Jewish musicians for the general public are described in

Troubadours 10:313-14
Süsskind von Trimberg 10:108-9 (G)

The chief articles on Jewish musicians of modern times are

MUSICAL ORGANIZATIONS AND THE JEWS 8:55-66

MUSICIANS, JEWISH 8:66-68

The biographies of Jewish musicians may be classified into the following groups:

Composers

Rossi, Salamone 9:230-31 (I)
Mendelssohn-Bartholdy, Felix 7:475-77 (G)
Goldmark, Karl 5:26-27 (A)
Halévy, Jacques 5:178-79 (F)
Mahler, Gustav 7:282-84 (A)
Meyerbeer, Giacomo 7:520-21 (G, I, F)
Moskowski, Moritz 8:22 (G, F)
Nachez, Tivadar 8:79-80 (F, US)
Nápravnik, Eduard 8:101 (A, Ru)
Nathan, Isaac 8:108 (E, Aus)
Offenbach, Jacques 8:285-86 (F)
Rubinstein, Anton 9:272 (Ru)
Wieniawski, Henri 10:515-16 (Po, F, Be, Ru)
Schönberg, Arnold 9:418-19 (A, US)
Milhaud, Darius 7:559-60 (F)
Dukas, Paul 3:608 (F)
Rathaus, Karol 9:81 (A, US)
Weill, Kurt 10:486-87 (G, US)
Toch, Ernst 10:259-60 (G, US)
Wellesz, Egon 10:499-500 (A, E)
Zemlinsky, Alexander 10:638 (A, G, US)
Korngold, Erich Wolfgang 6:457 (A, G, US)
Tansman, Alexander 10:171 (Po, US)

Castelnuovo-Tedesco, Mario 3:59-60 (I)
Weiner, Lazar 10:489 (US)
Weinberger, Jaromir 10:489 (Cz, US)
Cowen, Frederic H. 3:390-91 (E)
Rosenbloom, Sydney 9:211 (E, S Af)
Veprik, Alexander 10:405 (Ru)
Gniessin, Michael 4:628-29 (Ru)
Kreyn, Alexander 6:470-71 (Ru)
Bauer, Marion Eugenie 2:114 (US)
Blitzstein, Marc 2:394 (US)
Bloch, Ernest 2:397-99 (Swi, US)
Chasins, Abram 3:119-20 (US)
Copland, Aaron 3:365-66 (US)
Diamond, David Leo 3:559-60 (US)
Gershwin, George 4:589-91 (US)
Goldmark, Rubin 5:27 (US)
Gruenberg, Louis 5:108-9 (US)
Jacobi, Frederick 6:15-16 (US)
Saminsky, Lazare 9:339-40 (Ru, US)
Schuman, William Howard 9:430 (US)

Violinists

Ernst, Heinrich 4:154 (F, E)
David, Ferdinand 3:486 (G)
Joachim, Joseph 6:152-53 (G)
Kreisler, Fritz 6:469 (A, US)
Heifetz, Jascha 5:292-93 (Ru, US)
Szigeti, Joseph 10:145-46 (Hu, Swi, US)
Milstein, Nathan 7:564 (Ru, US)
Menuhin, Yehudi 7:491-92 (US)
Auer, Leopold 1:611 (Ru, US)
Zimbalist, Efrem 10:643 (Ru, US)
Flesch, Carl 4:326 (Ro, Ho, G, US)

Conductors

Costa, Michael 3:374 (I, E)
Dessoff, Felix Otto 3:544 (G)
Levi, Hermann 6:624 (G)
Dobrowen, Issai 3:581 (Ru, US)
Fried, Oskar 4:445-46 (G, Ru)
Golschmann, Vladimir 5:48 (F, US)
Koussevitsky, Serge 6:460-61 (Ru, F, US)
Kleiber, Erich 6:413 (G, Argentina)
Klemperer, Otto 6:417 (G, US)
Leinsdorf, Erich 6:601 (A, US)
Monteux, Pierre 7:632 (F, US)
Ormandy, Eugene 8:326 (US)
Polacco, Giorgio 8:562
  (I, E, Brazil, Argentina, US)
Reiner, Fritz 9:119 (Hu, G, US)
Rodzinski, Arthur 9:182 (Po, US)
Walter, Bruno 10:448 (G, A, US)
Colonne, Édouard 3:304 (F)
Damrosch, Leopold 3:453-54 (G, US)
Damrosch, Frank 3:453 (US)
Damrosch, Walter 3:454 (US)

Pianists

Heller, Stephen 5:309 (Hu, A, F)
Tausig, Karl 10:179 (Po, G)
Joseffy, Rafael 6:184-85 (G, US)
Hiller, Ferdinand 5:368 (G)

Friedberg, Carl 4:446 (G, US)
Friedman, Ignaz 4:456 (A, G)
Gabrilowitsch, Ossip 4:489-90 (Ru, G, US)
Godowsky, Leopold 5:8-9 (US, A)
Hess, Myra 5:345 (E)
Horowitz, Vladimir 5:460-61 (Ru, US)
Landowska, Wanda 6:529 (G, F, US)
Rubinstein, Artur 9:272 (Po, US)
Schnabel, Artur 9:411-12 (A, G, I, US)
Serkin, Rudolph 9:481 (A, US)

Vocalists

Hauser, Franz 5:251 (A, G)
Braham, John 2:492 (E)
Renaud, Maurice 9:134 (F)
Lucca, Pauline 7:228 (A, G, E)
Kurz, Selma 6:492 (A)
Jadlowker, Hermann 6:26 (G, Latvia, P)
Kipnis, Alexander 6:396 (G, US)
Schorr, Friedrich 9:423 (Hu, A, G, US)
List, Emanuel 7:84 (A, US, G)
Pauly, Rose 8:417 (G, US)
Sack, Erna 9:305 (G, US)
Raïsa, Rosa 9:68 (I, US)
Gluck, Alma 4:623 (US)
Braslau, Sophie 2:504 (US)
Rappold, Marie 9:76 (US)
Tokatyan, Armand 10:260-61 (I, US)
Peerce, Jan 8:422 (US)

Musicologists

Adler, Guido 1:93 (A)
Friedländer, Max 4:453 (G)
Hanslick, Edward 5:208 (A)
Leichtentritt, Hugo 6:600 (G, US)
Nettl, Paul 8:154 (Cz, US)
Sachs, Kurt 9:304 (G, F, US)
Schenker, Heinrich 9:396 (A)
Stefan, Paul 10:37 (A, F, Pt, US)
Schillinger, Josef 9:406 (Ru, US)
Ewen, David 4:200 (US)

Others

Popper, David, cellist 8:600 (A)
Da Ponte, Lorenzo, librettist 3:444-45
  (I, A, E, US)

OUTLINE 94: JEWS IN PHILOSOPHY

In addition to contributing to the development of philosophy in the Middle Ages (for which see the outline on JEWISH PHILOSOPHY), Jews have furthered the advance of modern philosophy both in the creation of new systems and in the exploration of the work of older philosophers.

The great names among the Jewish philosophers of modern times are

Spinoza, Baruch 10:5-8 (Ho)
Mendelssohn, Moses 7:471-74 (G)
Cohen, Herman 3:244-45 (G)

Bergson, Henri Louis 2:201-3 (F; for the circumstances of his death in 1941, *see* 4:384)

Husserl, Eduard 5:508 (G)

Noted Jewish scholars in philosophy, arranged in chronological order, are

Freudenthal, Jacob 4:443 (G)
Liebmann, Otto 7:56 (G)
Gomperz, Theodor 5:55 (A)
Simmel, Georg 9:542-43 (G)
Mauthner, Fritz 7:416 (G)
Alexander, Samuel 1:176 (E)
Joel, Karl 6:160-61 (G, Swi)
Brunschvicg, Léon 2:567 (F)
Neumark, David 8:161-62 (US)
Benda, Julien 2:162 (F)
Cassirer, Ernst 3:58-59 (G)
Lask, Emil 6:537 (G)
Misch, Georg 7:579-80 (G)
Cohen, Morris Raphael 3:252-53 (US)
Nelson, Leonard 8:149 (G)
Meyerson, Émile 7:523 (F)
Kallen, Horace Mayer 6:298 (US)
Guttmann, Julius (Judah) 5:136-37 (G, P)
Kroner, Richard 6:477 (G)
Husik, Isaac 5:507 (US)
Rosenzweig, Franz 9:225-26 (G)
Heinemann, Isaak 5:302 (G)
Edman, Irwin 3:627 (US)
Wolfson, Harry A. 10:560-62 (US)
Roth, Leon 9:232 (E)
Diesendruck, Zevi 3:564 (P, US)
Heschel, Abraham 5:344 (G, US)

OUTLINE 95: JEWS IN PUBLIC OFFICE

During the Middle Ages it was almost entirely in Moslem lands that Jews were called to public office. In modern times they were summoned to duty as the ministers of rulers; but it was only with the opportunities afforded by countries permeated by the spirit of liberty and equality that they began to serve in large numbers. Since the middle of the 19th century Jews have been active in every field of public service.

The comprehensive article on the subject is

PUBLIC OFFICE, JEWS IN 9:22-31

In ancient times, the only person worth mentioning is

Alexander, Tiberius Julius, procurator of Judea 1:174

Jews in public office up to 1800 include

Isaac, in the embassy of Charlemagne 5:589
Hasdai ibn Shaprut, diplomat 5:236
Samuel Hanagid, vizier 9:348-49
Abraham bar Hiyya, governor of a city 1:40-41
Abulafia, Samuel ben Meir, minister, 1:62
Abravanel, Isaac, minister and diplomat 1:53-54

Joseph Nasi, governor and diplomat 6:192-94
Eskenazi, Solomon Nathan, diplomat 4:165-66
Milan, Gabriel, governor of the Virgin Islands 7:558-59
Teixeira, Sampayo Diego, emissary of Sweden 10:189
Oppenheimer, Joseph Süss, chief minister of Württemberg 8:310-12

Those Jews who have served in modern times, classified by countries, are

Australia

Cohen, Harold Edward, minister 3:241
Cohen, Henry Isaac, minister 3:244
Isaacs, Isaac Alfred, minister and governor general 5:597-98

Austria

Glaser, Julius Anton, minister 4:617
Unger, Josef, minister 10:343
Adler, Victor, minister 1:97
Schueller, Richard, minister and envoy 9:427

Belgium

Hymans, Paul, minister 5:516
May, Paul, diplomat 7:418-19

British Empire

Disraeli, Benjamin, prime minister 3:570-73
Pirbright, Lord, member of the Privy Council 8:541
Reading, Rufus, Marquess of, chief justice, viceroy of India 9:90-92
Samuel, 1st Viscount, minister, High Commissioner for Palestine 9:350-51
Jessel, Sir George, solicitor general and master of the rolls 6:82
Hore-Belisha, Leslie, minister 5:453-54

Canada

Croll, David Arnold, minister 3:423

Czechoslovakia

Meissner, Alfred, minister 7:448
Winter, Lev, minister 10:530-31

Denmark

Brandes, Carl Edvard, minister 2:500

France

Crémieux, Isaac Adolphe, minister 3:407
Goudchaux, Michel, minister 5:75
Fould, Achille, minister 4:360-61
Blum, Léon, minister and premier 2:416-17

NOTE—At the time the article was written it was reported that Blum had escaped to England. Subsequently it was learned that he had remained in France. He was arrested, but the trial at Riom at which he was accused of betraying France, was halted when it degenerated into a farce. Nothing is known of Blum's fate after the Germans occupied Vichy France in 1941.

Bokanowski, Maurice, minister 2:442-43
Klotz, Lucien Louis, minister 6:418-19
Mandel, Georges, minister 7:316-18

Germany

Eisner, Kurt, Bavarian premier 4:41
Friedberg, Heinrich von, Prussian minister 4:446
Friedenthal, Karl Rudolph, Prussian minister 4:447
Hilferding, Rudolf, Reich minister 5:360
Rathenau, Walther, Reich minister and diplomat 9:81-82

Holland

Asser, Tobias Michael Carel, minister 1:555
Godefroi, Michael H., minister 5:8

Hungary

Böhm, Vilmos, minister and commander-in-chief of the army 2:442
Hazai, Samu, minister and general 5:259
Kunfi, Zsigmond, minister 6:488
Szende, Pal, minister 10:143
Vázsonyi, Vilmos, minister 10:397-98
Schwimmer, Rozsika, envoy 9:439-40
Gallia, Béla, Supreme Court justice 4:502
Löw, Tibor, chief justice, Court of Appeals 7:216

Italy

Luzzatti, Luigi, prime minister 7:244-45
Morpurgo, Elio, minister 7:654
Morpurgo, Emilio, minister 7:654
Mortara, Lodovico, first president, Supreme Court of Appeals 7:657
Ottolenghi, Giuseppe, minister 8:337
Romanin, Jacur Leone, minister 9:186
Wollemborg, Leone, minister 10:563
Artom, Ernesto, diplomat 1:516
Artom, Isacco, minister and diplomat 1:516

Latvia

Meierowics, Zigrids, prime minister and diplomat 7:443

New Zealand

Myers, Michael, chief justice 8:72
Vogel, Sir Julius, prime minister 10:430

Poland

Askenazy, Simon, diplomat 1:551-52
Schwarzbart, Izak Ignacy, National Council in Exile 9:436-37
Zigelbojm, Samuel, National Council in Exile 10:642-43

Russia

Trotsky, Leon Davidovich, commissar and commander-in-chief, Red Army 10:312-13
Kamenev, Lev Borisovich, envoy at Brest-Litovsk, member of the Political Bureau 6:302
Sverdlov, Yakov Mikhailovich, chairman Central Executive Committee and of the Soviets 10:110-11
Kaganovich, Lazar Moiseivich, commissar 6:279

Litvinoff, Maxim, minister and diplomat 7:143-45
Lozovsky, Solomon, vice-commissar 7:221-22
Joffe, Adolf Abramovitch, diplomat 6:162-63
Oumansky, Constantin, diplomat 8:338-39
Maisky, Ivan, diplomat 7:297

Turkey

Kiamil Pasha, vizier 6:379

United States

Diplomats

Belmont, August 2:153
Bernstein, Herman 2:235-36
Einstein, Lewis 4:34
Elkus, Abram L. 4:83-84
Guggenheim, Harry F. 5:122-23
Kaufman, David E. 6:341
Kornfeld, Joseph E. (d. 1943) 6:456
Morgenthau, Henry, Sr. 7:646-48
Morris, Ira Nelson 7:655-56
Peixotto, Benjamin Franklin 8:422-23
Steinhardt, Laurence A. 10:46-47
Straus, Jesse Isidor 10:79

Cabinet Members

Straus, Oscar Solomon (also diplomat) 10:77-79
Morgenthau, Henry, Jr. 7:648-50

Judiciary

Brandeis, Louis D. (d. 1941) 2:495-97
Cardozo, Benjamin Nathan 3:39-42
Frankfurter, Felix 4:407-10
Lehman, Irving, chief justice, New York State Court of Appeals 6:595-96

Senators

Benjamin, Judah P. (also minister of the Confederacy) 2:181-84
Guggenheim, Simon (d. 1941) 5:121-22
Jonas, Benjamin Franklin 6:179
Rayner, Isidor 9:87-88
Simon, Joseph 9:547
Yulee, David Levy 10:621

Governors of States and Territories

Alexander, Moses 1:175-76
Bamberger, Simon 2:61
Emanuel, David 4:95
Gruening, Ernest 5:110
Hahn, Michael 5:166-67
Horner, Henry 5:455-56
Lehman, Herbert H. 6:592-95
Meier, Julius L. 7:442-43
Ratner, Payne Harry (of Jewish descent) 9:84
Seligman, Arthur 9:466-67
Sholtz, David 9:518
Solomon, Edward S. 9:639

Miscellaneous

Baruch, Bernard M., war-time administrator, 2:98-99

Lasker, Albert D., chairman, United States Shipping Board 6:537-38

Meyer, Eugene, Jr., War Finance Corporation, Federal Reserve Board, Reconstruction Finance Corporation 7:515-16

Rowe, Leo S., director-general, Pan-American Union 9:266-67

Frank, Jerome New, chairman, Securities Exchange Commission, and federal judge 4:393-94

OUTLINE 96: JEWS AS SOLDIERS

Jewish soldiers have a long record of prowess, beginning with the heroes of Bible times and continuing down to the great wars of the present generation. They have served in the armies of every country, and in many they have achieved positions of high rank and numerous military honors.

The comprehensive article on the subject is

SOLDIER, JEW AS 9:594-633

The following are noteworthy Jewish soldiers of modern times, arranged according to countries and in chronological order:

United States
Colonial and Revolutionary Period
Hart, Aaron 5:223-24
Sheftall, Mordecai 9:499-500
Franks, David Salisbury 4:418
Franks, Isaac 4:417-18
Cardozo, David Nunez 3:42
Nones, Benjamin 8:232-33
From the Revolution to the Civil War

> NOTE—Since the article on Soldier, Jew as, was written, a new name has come to light, that of Simon M. Levy, who fought ably at Maumee Rapids in 1794, was one of two early graduates of West Point in 1802, and served at Fort Jackson, Ga., until 1805; he died two years later.

Massias, Abraham A. 7:408
Noah, Samuel 8:227
Levy, Aaron 7:6
Mordecai, Alfred (Senior) 7:643
De Leon, David Camden 3:499

Civil War

Einstein, Max 4:34-35
Cohn, Abraham 3:257
Frauenthal, Max 4:426
Greenhut, Joseph Benedict 5:98
Blumenberg, Leopold 2:418
Knefler, Frederick 6:420
Moise, Edwin Warren 7:611-12
Mordecai, Alfred (Junior) 7:643-44
Moses, Raphael J. 8:14-15
Newman, Leopold C. 8:212
Solomon, Edward S. 9:639

From the End of the Civil War to 1943
Foreman, Milton J. 4:356-57
Davis, Abel 3:490-91
Prager, Benjamin 8:613
Dreben, Sam 3:595
Lawton, Samuel T. 6:565
Adler, Julius Ochs 1:95
Gumpertz, Sydney Gustave 5:129
Kaufman, Benjamin 6:340
Krotoshinsky, Abraham 6:478
Ross, Barney 9:229

In the United States Navy
Ordronaux, John 8:320
Harby, Levi Myers 5:213-14
Levy, Uriah Phillips 7:17-18
Etting, Henry 4:189
Hartstein, Henry Julius 5:234
Marix, Adolph 7:358
Moritz, Albert 7:650-51
Strauss, Joseph 10:82-83
Josephthal, Louis Maurice 6:197
Ellsberg, Edward 4:87
Moreell, Ben 7:645

England
Schomberg, Sir Alexander 9:417
Montefiore, Joshua 7:630
Nathan, Sir Matthew 8:109
Harris, Sir David 5:218
Kisch, Frederick H. (d. 1943) 6:402-3
Smith, Israel (Issy) 9:572-73
Gee, Robert 4:519

France
Masséna, André 7:407-8
Moch, Jules 7:605-6
Levi, Camille Baruch 6:623
Valabrègue, Mardochée Georges 10:389
Weiller, André 10:487
Geismar, Gédéon 4:523-24
Meyer, Samuel 7:518

Germany
Burg, Meno 2:590
Manuel, Esther 7:335
Mossner, Walter von 8:21

Italy
Guastalla, Enrico 5:114-15
Scott, Charles Alexander 9:447
Ottolenghi, Giuseppe 8:337
Segre, Roberto 9:461-62

Russia
Mekhlis, Lev Zakharovich 7:448-49
Smushkevich, Iakov V. 9:575-76

Australia
Monash, Sir John 7:617
Rosenthal, Sir Charles 9:218-19
Keyser, Leonard 6:374

Other Countries

Berkowicz, Josef (Poland) 2:204
Hart, Benjamin (Canada) 5:224
Singer, Joseph (Austria) 9:556-57
Borovsky, Isidor (South America and Persia) 2:478
Mazar Pasha (England and Turkey) 7:427
Magyar Mahmoud Pasha (Hungary and Turkey) 7:280
Brie, Luis H. (Argentina) 2:528
Brociner, Moritz (Roumania) 2:537
Sommer, Emil von (Austria) 9:645
Cohen, Maurice A. (China) 3:251-52
Frizis, Mordecai (Greece) 4:463

For the work of Jewish army chaplains, *see* Chaplains, Jewish § 1. 3:111-12

The following articles deal with Jewish military organizations:

Irgun Tzebai Leumi 5:586
Jewish Lads' Brigade 6:133
Jewish Legion 6:133-34

OUTLINE 97: JEWS IN THE THEATRE

Jews began to participate in the theatre about the time it began to develop into its modern form. They have contributed a number of distinguished playwrights, producers and actors to the modern stage and to its allied forms of motion pictures and radio. At the same time there has been a development of the Hebrew and Yiddish stages, and the latter in particular has given many stars to the current theatre.

The comprehensive article on the subject is

THEATRE 10:208-39

The following are the most important Jewish participants in the modern theatre, arranged in chronological order by language groups and countries:

A. Playwrights

French

Bernstein, Henry 2:235
Bernard, Tristan 2:225

English (England)

Pinero, Arthur Wing 8:534-35
Sutro, Alfred 10:110

English (United States)

Harby, Isaac 5:213
Noah, Mordecai Manuel 8:226-27
Belasco, David (also producer) 2:145-47
Klein, Charles 6:413-14
Pollock, Channing 8:583
Rice, Elmer 9:156
Kaufman, George S. 6:341-42
Odets, Clifford 8:283-84

Behrman, Samuel N. 2:138
Hart, Moss 5:228-29
Kingsley, Sidney 6:393
Hellman, Lillian F. 5:311-12

Hungarian

Molnar, Ferenc 7:614-15

German

Schnitzler, Arthur 9:413-15
Werfel, Franz 10:501-2
Fulda, Ludwig 4:470
Beer-Hofmann, Richard 2:135-36

For Hebrew and Yiddish playwrights, *see* the outlines on HEBREW and YIDDISH LITERATURE.

B. Producers

1. On the Stage

English

Lumley, Benjamin (England) 7:235-36
Frohman, Charles 4:463-64
Frohman, Daniel 4:464-65
Erlanger, Abraham L. 4:153
Shubert, Lee 9:521
Harris, Sam H. 5:220
Harris, Jed 5:218
Shumlin, Herman E. 9:523

Of special interest in this connection is the career of

Hammerstein, Oscar 5:198-99

German

Reinhardt, Max 9:120   Brahm, Otto 2:492-93

2. Motion Pictures

England

Korda, Alexander 6:453-54

France

Benoit-Levy, Jean 2:186

Hungary

Biró, Lajos 2:372
Lengyel, Menyhért 6:605-6

Russia

Eisenstein, Sergei M. 4:39-40

United States

Zukor, Adolph 10:676-77
Loew, Marcus 7:160-161
Fox, William 4:364
Mayer, Louis B. 7:424-25

Laemmle, Carl 6:507-8
Goldwyn, Samuel 5:42
Fleischer, Max 4:323-24
Warner 10:460-61
Selznick, David O. 9:472

3. Actors

(where actors have been prominent in more than one branch of the theatre, they are placed under that in which they are best known)

1. On the Stage

France

Felix, Elisa Rachel (Rachel) 4:272
Bernhardt, Sarah 2:228-29
Berr, Georges 2:239

Germany and Austria

Dawison, Bogumil 3:493
Dessoir, Ludwig 3:545
Sonnenthal, Adolf Ritter von 9:650
Barnay, Ludwig 2:86-87
Ludwig, Maximilian 7:232

Pallenberg, Max 8:380
Beregi, Oszkár 2:195
Pohl, Max 8:559
Kortner, Fritz 6:458
Mannheim, Lucie 7:332
Mosheim, Grete 8:16
Bergner, Elizabeth 2:201

Holland

Bouwmeester, Louis 2:485-86
Van Rijk, Esther de Boer 10:394-95

United States

Menken, Ada Isaacs 7:485-86
Warfield, David 10:460
Mann, Louis 7:325
Jolson, Al 6:176

Reed, Florence (of Jewish descent) 9:101
Menken, Helen 7:486
Cantor, Eddie 3:18

Yiddish

Adler 1:85-87
Thomashefsky, Boris 10:245-46
Schildkraut, Rudolph 9:405
Schwartz, Maurice 9:434-35
Ben-Ami, Jacob 2:156
Picon, Molly 8:530

Hebrew

Habimah 5:143-44
Of special interest is the question of the Jewish ancestry of
Kean, Edmund 6:350-51

2. Motion Pictures (all United States)

Actors

Chaplin, Charles S. 3:112-13
Robinson, Edward G. 9:175-76

Muni, Paul 8:35
Sidney, Sylvia 9:528
Rainer, Luise 9:68

Directors

Lubitsch, Ernst 7:225
Curtiz, Michael 3:435-36
Mankiewicz, Herman J. 7:324
Wyler, William 10:581
Kanin, Garson 6:304

C. Radio (all United States)

Sarnoff, David 9:371
Paley, William S. 8:379

Brice, Fanny 2:526
Benny, Jack 2:186
Berg, Gertrude 2:198

D. Dramatic Critics

Cohen, Alfred J. (United States) 3:237
Eloesser, Arthur (Germany) 4:89
Kerr, Alfred (Germany) 6:365-66
Nathan, George Jean (United States) 8:107-8

The following organization is an association of Jews in the theatrical business:
Jewish Theatrical Guild 6:143

OUTLINE 98:

JEWS IN TRAVEL AND EXPLORATION

Travel and exploration came naturally to Jews. Scattered as they were throughout the world, they needed to maintain constant communication with one another, and necessarily undertook long journeys to accomplish this. Furthermore, whereas non-Jews feared to leave the safety of their own people to go among strangers, the Jews could always count upon the assistance and hospitality of their own correligionists in another country. When persecution assailed them, the Jews were always eager to seek new lands in which they might find freedom. Hence they became bearers of royal messages, pioneers of the discoveries of the 15th and 16th cenuturies, and explorers in modern times.

The story of Jewish travelers is found in

TRAVELERS AND TRAVEL LITERATURE 10:297

Among the early Jewish travelers were

Isaac 5:589 (G)
Eldad Hadani 4:46
Benjamin of Tudela 2:180 (S)
Pethahiah of Regensburg 8:471 (G)
Farhi, Estori ha- 4:247 (F, S, P)

Among the Jews who contributed through their scientific achievements to the discoveries of the 15th century and after were

Ibn Wakar, Josph ben Abraham 5:531 (S)
Bonfils, Immanuel ben Jacob 2:452-53 (F)
Cresques, Jehudah 3:409-10 (S)
Zacuto, Abraham ben Samuel 10:622 (S, Pt, Tunisia)
Vecinho, Joseph 10:398 (Pt)

A summary of this contribution is contained in

CARTOGRAPHY 3:53

A history of Jewish explorers is given in

EXPLORATION AND EXPLORERS 4:215-17

The following are the most important Jewish explorers, divided according to geographical regions:

The Americas

Columbus, Christopher 3:306-10 (the article discusses the assistance which he received from Jews, as well as his own possibly Jewish origin)

Torres, Luis de 10:281 (S)

Gama, Gaspard da 4:505 (India, Pt)

Bernheimer, Charles Leopold 2:230-31 (US)

Radin, Paul 9:65 (US)

Kahn, Morton Charles 6:289 (US)

Herskovits, Melville Jean 5:331 (US)

Popper, Julius 8:601 (Ro)

The Near East

Cherni, Joseph Judah 3:132 (Ru)

Glaser, Eduard 4:616-17 (A)

Müller, David Heinrich von 8:33-34 (A)

Vámbéry, Arminius 10:390-91 (Hu)

Merzbacher, Gottfried 7:497 (G)

Central Asia

Stein, Sir Marc Aurel 10:39-40 (E)

Elias, Ney 4:68 (E)

Northern Asia

Jochelson, Vladimir 6:159 (Ru)

Sternberg, Lev Yakovlevich 10:60 (Ru)

Laufer, Berthold 6:551-52 (G, US)

Huth, Georg 5:508-9 (G)

The Far East

Teixeira, Pedro 10:189 (Pt)

Bernstein, Henrich Agathon 2:235 (G)

Fenichel, Samuel 4:274 (Hu)

Loria, Lamberto 7:194 (I)

Seligman, Charles Gabriel 9:467 (E)

Africa

Emin Pasha, Mehmed 4:100 (G)

Binger, Louis Gustave 2:355 (F)

Foa, Edouard 4:346 (F)

Burchardt, Hermann 2:590 (G)

Isaacs, Nathaniel 5:599-600 (S Af)

Franchetti, Raimondo 4:386 (I)

Straus, Sarah Lavanburg 10:79 (US)

The Arctic Regions

Lyons, Israel 7:256 (E)

Hayes, Isaac Israel 5:254 (US)

Bessels, Emil 2:248 (G)

Israel, Edward 5:618 (US)

Heilprin, Angelo 5:295-96 (US)

Samoilovich, Rudolph L. 9:340 (Ru)

The following are Jewish travelers of more modern times:

Azulai, Hayim Joseph David 1:655 (P, Egypt, I)

Benjamin II 2:178 (Ro)

Noah, Mordecai Manuel 8:226-27 (US)

Baruch ben Samuel of Safed 2:97 (P)

Romanelli, Samuel Aaron 9:186 (I)

Slouschz, Nahum 9:570-71 (Ru, P)

Salmon, Alexander 9:319-20 (E)

OUTLINE 99: JEWS IN VARIOUS FIELDS

In addition to the specific fields to which separate outlines are devoted, there are a number of other departments of scholarship or scientific research in which Jews have played a part. The most important Jewish contributors in these fields are grouped together in the present outline under main heads and in chronological order.

Agriculturists

Lubin, David 7:223 (US, I)

Lipman, Jacob Goodale 7:73-74 (US)

Anthropologists

Boas, Franz 2:430-32 (US)

Bogoraz, Vladimir 2:439 (Ru)

Seligman, Charles Gabriel 9:467 (E)

Fishberg, Maurice 4:319-20 (US)

Criminologists

Lombroso, Cesare 7:169-70 (I)

Glueck, Sheldon 4:627 (US)

Engineers

Gaunse, Joachim 4:518 (E)

Sutro, Adolph 10:109-10 (US)

Steinmetz, Charles Proteus 10:49 (US)

Strauss, Joseph Baerman 10:83 (US)

Ellsberg, Edward 4:87 (US)

Moisseiff, Leon S. 7:613 (US)

Kotin, Joseph 6:460 (Ru)

Geologists

Lévy, Auguste-Michel 7:8 (F)

Goldschmidt, Victor Moritz 5:32-33 (N)

Indologists and Sanskritologists

Goldstücker, Theodor 5:40-41 (E)

Lévi, Sylvain 6:626-27 (F)

Winternitz, Moritz 10:531 (E, Cz, India)

Orientalists

Munk, Salomon 8:37-38 (F)

Loewe, Louis 7:161-62 (G, E)

Oppert, Julius 8:314-15 (F)

Vámbéry, Arminius 10:390-91 (Hu)

Derenbourg, Hartwig 3:540-41 (F)

Halévy, Joseph 5:179 (T, F)

Goldziher, Ignaz 5:42-43 (Hu)

Darmesteter, James 3:472 (F)

Müller, David Heinrich von 8:33-34 (A)

Mahler, Ede 7:282 (Hu, A)

Kunos, Ignác 6:488-89 (Hu)

Gottheil, Richard J. H. 5:70-71 (US)

Ember, Aaron 4:96-97 (US)

Jastrow, Morris, Jr. 6:45-46 (US)

Popper, William 8:601 (US)

Horovitz, Joseph 5:457 (G)

Mittwoch, Eugen (d. 1942) 7:591 (G, E)

Philologists

Lehrs, Karl 6:599 (G)

Benfey, Theodor 2:172 (G)

Ascoli, Graziadio 1:535-36 (I)

Mussafia, Adolfo 8:68 (A)
Bréal, Michel 2:516 (F)
Darmesteter, Arsène 3:471 (F)
Simonyi, Zsigmond 9:551 (Hu)
Munkácsi, Bernát 8:39-40 (Hu)
Halász, Ignác 5:175-76 (Hu)
Morpurgo, Salomone 7:655 (I)
Margolis, Max L. 7:354-55 (US)
Levias, Caspar 6:628 (US)
Blondheim, David S. 2:405-6 (US)
Luria, Max A. 7:239 (US)

Physicists
Riess, Peter Theophil 9:162-63 (G)
Michelson, Albert A. 7:532-34 (US)
Hertz, Heinrich 5:332 (G)
Volterra, Vito 10:433 (I)
Lippmann, Gabriel 7:75 (F)
Franck, James 4:387-88 (G, US)
Joffe, Abram F. 6:162 (Ru)
Einstein, Albert 4:29-33 (G, Swi, US)
Bohr, Niels 2:442 (D)

Psychologists
Münsterberg, Hugo 8:40-41 (G, US)
Jastrow, Joseph 6:44 (US)
Stern, William 10:60 (G, US)
Myers, Charles Samuel 8:70-71 (E)
Wertheimer, Max 10:505 (G, US)
Kohs, Samuel Calmin 6:436 (US)
Lewin, Kurt 7:22 (G, US)
Lazarsfeld, Paul F. 6:568 (A, US)

For additional names in these fields, *see*

Science and Invention 9:440-45

OUTLINE 100: NOTEWORTHY JEWS

In addition to the names listed in the previous outlines, there are a number of other Jews who are worth knowing because of their achievements in various fields. They are listed here in alphabetical order.

Abrahams, Israel (1858-1925), English scholar 1:47-48
Abravanel, Judah (1460-1525), Italian philosopher, physician and poet 1:54-55
Acosta, Uriel (1585-1640), Spanish and Netherlands religious dissenter 1:72-74
Adler, Cyrus (1863-1940), American educator and religious leader 1:88-89
Ashkenazi, Zebi Hirsch (1660-1718), Polish and German Talmudist 1:544-45
Barros Basto, Arthur Carlos de (b. 1887), Portuguese leader of the revival of Judaism among the Marranos 2:92-93
Ben Jehudah, Eliezer (1857-1922), Palestinian pioneer of modern Hebrew as a spoken language 2:159

Bloch, Ivan S. (1836-1901), Russian promoter of world peace 2:399-400
Borochov, Ber (1881-1917), Russian and American theoretician of the Poale Zion movement 2:476-77
Buber, Martin (b. 1878), German scholar and collector of Hasidic tales 2:569-70
Cohen (1744 on), prominent American family 3:233-36
Cutler, Harry (1875-1920), American communal leader 3:437
Disraeli, Isaac (1766-1848), English writer 3:574
Elijah Vilna (1720-97), Polish Talmudist and educator 4:76-77
Etting (1737 on), early American family 4:186-90
Frankel, Zacharias (1801-75), German rabbi and leader of Conservative Judaism 4:399-400
Fried, Alfred H. (1864-1921), Austrian champion of world peace 4:445
Friedländer, David (1750-1834), German religious reformer 4:452-53
Gaster, Moses (1856-1939), Roumanian and English rabbi and scholar 4:516-17
Gershom ben Judah (960-1040), Talmudist and communal leader 4:588
Glückel of Hameln (1647-1724), German writer of memoirs 4:624-25
Goldsmid (1765 on), prominent English family 5:33-35
Gratz (1756 on), pioneer American family 5:85-87
Hevesi, Simon (b. 1868), Hungarian chief rabbi 5:350-51
Hirsch, Emil Gustav (1851-1923), American rabbi and civic leader 5:373-75
Josel of Rosheim (1480-1554), German representative of the Jews to the emperor 6:185-87
Kohler, Kaufmann (1843-1926), American rabbi, theologian and scholar 6:428-30
Kohler, Max James (1871-1934), American jurist and historian 6:431-32
Kohut, George Alexander (1874-1933), American author and scholar 6:437-38
Kohut, Rebekah (b. 1864), American educator and communal worker 6:438-39
Kook, Abraham Isaac (1864-1935), Palestinian chief rabbi 6:448-49
Lampronti, Isaac ben Samuel (1679-1756), Italian rabbi and encyclopedist 6:519-20
Landau, Ezekiel (1713-93), Polish and Bohemian Halachist 6:522-23
Levy, Asser (d. 1681), first American Jewish citizen 7:7-8
Loewi, Otto (b. 1873), German pharmacologist and Nobel Prize winner 7:165
Luzzatto, Samuel David (1800-65), Italian scholar 7:247-49
Marshall, Louis (1856-1929), American communal and civic leader 7:380-85
Mendes, Henry Pereira (1852-1937), American rabbi 7:479-80
Montefiore, Claude G. (1858-1938), English scholar and religious leader 7:628-29

Montefiore, Moses (1784-1885), English philanthropist and communal leader 7:630-31
Morais, Sabato (1823-97), American rabbi and leader in Conservative Judaism 7:638-40
Philipson, David (b. 1862), American rabbi and author 8:488-89
Rabbenu Tam (1100-71), French Talmudic authority 9:48
Reinach, Salomon (1858-1932), French historian of religion 9:117-18
Revel, Bernard (1885-1940), American scholar and Orthodox Jewish leader 9:146-47
Ricardo, David (1772-1823), English economist 9:155-56
Rosenman, Samuel Irving (b. 1896), American judge and political adviser 9:215-16
Rosenwald, Julius (1862-1932), American merchant and philanthropist 9:222-24
Schecter, Solomon (1847-1915), English and American scholar and leader of Conservative Judaism 9:393-95

Schulman, Samuel (b. 1864), American rabbi and theologian of the Reform Movement 9:428-30
Seixas, Gershom Mendez (1745-1816), American rabbi and patriot 9:462-63
Steinschneider, Moritz (1816-1907), German scholar 10:49-50
Straus (1850 on), American family 10:74-81
Sulzberger, Cyrus L. (1858-1932), American civic and communal leader 10:98-99
Sulzberger, Mayer (1843-1925), American communal leader 10:100-1
Touro, Judah (1775-1854), American philanthropist 10:285-86
Trumpeldor, Joseph (1880-1920), Russian and Palestinian soldier and Zionist leader 10:315-16
Untermyer, Samuel (1858-1940), American lawyer and communal worker 10:379
Warburg (1667 on), German, Scandinavian, English and American family 10:452-58
Zunz, Leopold (1794-1886), German scholar 10:677-79

INDEX